When **Not** to Build

When **Not** to Build

An Architect's Unconventional Wisdom for the Growing Church

Ray Bowman

with Eddy Hall

Foreword by Charles Arn

BAKER BOOK HOUSE
Grand Rapids, Michigan 49516

Portions of this book originally appeared in *Leadership*, *The Leadership Guide to Church Supplies*, *The Clergy Journal*, and *The Preacher's Magazine*.

Unless otherwise noted, Scripture quotations are from *The Living Bible*, copyright 1971, Tyndale House Publishers, Wheaton, Illinois. Scripture quotations designated NRSV are from the *New Revised Standard Version Bible*, copyright 1989, Division of Christian Education of the National Council of the Churches of Christ in the United States of America.

ISBN: 0-8010-1031-4

Sixth printing, September 1997

Printed in the United States of America

For information about academic books, resources for Christian leaders, and all new releases available from Baker Book House, visit our web site:
http://www.bakerbooks.com

To
James N. Posey
who brought us together
and without whom this book
would not have been written

Contents

When It's Time to Build

Conclusion

Foreword

Let me share a puzzle with you. It's a puzzle that stumped me for years. I knew there had to be an answer, but each time I tried to solve it, I became more and more frustrated. Only recently did I experience the "Aha!" that comes with a solution, and then it was only when someone more enlightened than I showed me the answer.

Here are the instructions. Connect the nine dots below using only four straight lines without lifting your pencil from the paper. Simple, right? Try it.

If you have seen the puzzle before and been shown the "secret solution," it's easy. If you are seeing it for the first time, you probably wonder how, or whether, it can be solved.

Here's a secret that can help you solve the problem. It's the same secret Ray Bowman has used in his wide experience of consulting with churches and the one he brings so insightfully to this new book. The secret is: *Don't look for the obvious solution.*

Still stuck? So are a lot of pastors of growing churches when it comes to accommodating the increasing number of people coming to their church. The obvious answer is to build. The wrong answer, for most, is to build.

Can such a paradox be true? Yes. And it won't be the first time.

Jesus, of course, used paradoxes to communicate many insights into the Christian faith:

If your enemy is hungry, give him food.

To be rich, give away your possessions.

To gain your life, lose it.

As I have observed how, when, where, and why churches grow across North America, the paradoxes of growth have also fascinated me:

To attract more people, raise membership requirements.

To grow a group, divide it.

To accommodate your growth in attendance, don't build.

Ray Bowman takes this latter paradox of church growth and explains why it is so. This unusual and perceptive book will bring you the "Aha!" experience that will turn night into day, frustration into insight.

The secret: *Don't look for the obvious solution.*

Oh, yes, the puzzle.

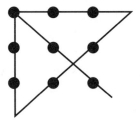

Try it with your friends sometime. Try it on a pastor or lay leader who is considering building a new sanctuary or educational wing. Then give him a copy of this book for the "secret solution."

Charles Arn, President
Church Growth, Inc.
Monrovia, California

Introduction

Fifteen Questions Before You Begin

Sunday mornings your worship space is filled to 90 percent capacity. The older teen and young married classes have standing room only. The fellowship hall can no longer seat everyone at once during your potluck dinners. Obviously, it's time to build.

Or is it?

For most churches in this situation, the answer is no. Certainly such a church has urgent facility needs, but a major building program is only one of many options for meeting those needs. Rarely is it the best one.

When a church asks me to help them assess their building needs, I often ask the pastor and board members to fill out a questionnaire to help identify motivations for building and gauge the congregation's need and readiness for a major building program.

If you think the time may have come for your church to build, answer each of the following questions *yes, no,* or *maybe.*

_____ 1. Do you expect a new building to attract new people to the church?

_____ 2. Is it your goal to design a building that will inspire people to worship?

_____ 3. Do you expect your members to be more motivated to reach out to others once you have a new building?

_____ 4. Do you think a building program will motivate your people to give more generously to the work of the church?

_____ 5. Do you expect the building program to unify your people behind a significant challenge?

_____ 6. Do you hope that a building program will involve more people in the work of the church?

_____ 7. Do you see the building as a way to make a statement to the community about the church's importance?

_____ 8. Do you hope that a new building will help your people take more pride in their church?

_____ 9. Do you need a larger sanctuary so the entire congregation can worship together at one time?

_____ 10. Do you need to add more educational space so all your classes can meet at once?

_____ 11. Is it possible that your space needs could be met through more creative use of your present facilities, such as converting space to multiple use, changing furnishings, scheduling services and ministries at alternate times, or using off-campus meeting space?

_____ 12. Are you still paying debt on your last building?

_____ 13. Would you have to borrow a major part of the finances for a building program?

_____ 14. Would payment for the project depend on the church's future growth?

_____ 15. To help pay for the building, would you explore ways to cut spending on your present ministry programs or staffing?

Now, add up your answers. Every *yes* or *maybe* is a possible reason not to build, to delay building, or to seek another more appropriate solution through prayer, research, and re-evaluation.

Questions 1 through 8 relate to motivations for building. These issues are discussed in part 1 of this book, "The Principle of

Focus." Questions 9 through 11 deal with how best to meet space needs, the subject of part 2, "The Principle of Use." Questions 12 through 15 address financial readiness, which is covered in part 3, "The Principle of Provision."

It is probably already obvious how some of these fifteen issues should influence your decision to build soon, wait a while, or pursue alternatives. By the time you finish studying the first ten chapters of this book, you should understand clearly why your answer to each of these questions is important to your facility decisions.

The principles of focus, use, and provision can help your church avoid a premature or unnecessary building program, but if your church continues to grow, the time to build probably will come. Part 4 of the book, "When It's Time to Build," explains who should plan your new building (most churches ask the wrong people to do it), and describes innovative design features that can make your facility a more effective ministry tool.

Finally, an appendix turns the whole book into a working handbook for the congregation that is ready to develop a master facility plan.

If you are looking for ways to fine-tune the church's traditional ways of thinking about, using, and paying for church buildings, this book will not answer your questions. It does not offer traditional solutions.

But if you are among the growing number who uneasily wonder if the church spends too much of its time, money, and energy on buildings; if you feel there must be a better way, a way that would free the church to redirect many of its human and financial resources to meeting the needs of people; if you have ever wished someone could show you and your congregation a proven, workable plan for doing that, then read on. This book is for you.

1

Confessions of a Surprised Architect

When a suburban Philadelphia congregation asked me to design a thousand-seat sanctuary, that's exactly what I intended to do. They had called me for the usual reasons. Their sanctuary was full and they were running out of educational space. It was time to build.

To determine how best to design their facility, I first met with the church board for four hours on a Saturday morning. Next I spent several days studying the church's ministries, finances, and use of facilities. Then I met with the church-growth committee. Finally, I was sure I had the facts I needed to draft my proposal.

I met with the board again the following Saturday. "What you really need to build," I announced, "is a storage shed."

Had the church invited me a year and a half earlier, I would have designed a thousand-seat sanctuary and cheered them on. "The building will bring more people to Christ," I would have said. "Its beauty will draw you closer to God. People will notice you're here and that you're an important part of the community."

During thirty years of designing church buildings, I had heard all these claims from pastors and church boards and saw no reason not to accept their assumption that bigger buildings translated into greater ministry. But then my life took a surprising turn that made me look at the church through new eyes and forced me to rethink the conventional wisdom that had guided three decades of work.

In 1979 if anyone had suggested I would soon change careers, I probably would have laughed. I had studied to be an architect, spent all my working life as an architect, and after building my own firm and spending twenty-six years as a principal had no intention of ever being anything but an architect.

Then one day as I was driving to our Twin Falls, Idaho, office to meet with one of my partners, a thought came to me as clearly as if someone had entered the car and spoken to me: "There's going to be a big change in your life, and it's going to involve your profession." I recognized the voice. When I got home, I told my wife, Sally, about it, then promptly forgot it.

Three weeks later I had a totally unexpected opportunity to leave my architectural firm when one of my partners, over lunch, offered to buy my stock. I had absolutely no idea what prompted his offer. When I told Sally about it, she said, "No way!" But as we prayed about it, both Sally and I felt we should accept.

"But, Lord," I said, "then I'll have no work and no income. What am I supposed to do?"

God's answer was clear even if a bit sketchy on details: "I'll show you what kind of work you are to do and give you all the work you can handle." On the strength of that promise I accepted my partner's offer and left behind an established career for an unknown future.

The day after I signed the papers dissolving my association with the firm, Sally and I were on our way to Canada for our first consulting job. A church in Red Deer, Alberta, had asked me to conduct a feasibility study to determine whether they should renovate their existing building or relocate to a larger site. Though it was just my first day to wear my consultant hat, I felt at once the difference it made. Even if the church were to decide to build, I knew I would not be their architect. I don't suppose the possibility of advising a church *not* to build had ever crossed my mind before. But at Red Deer, for the first time, it was a live option.

When I was an architect my job had been to follow instructions, to design whatever kind of building the church asked for. When I became a consultant, though, my job changed. I had to advise the church on what was best for the church, and that meant looking at the big picture. I analyzed the church's finances. I charted growth patterns. I studied utilization patterns of the existing building. At Red Deer I ended up advising the church to remodel and grow right where it was.

But the biggest surprise of that consultation came as I was about to leave. "Ray," the pastor said, "do you know what you are?"

"No," I answered, "I really don't."

"What you are," he said, "is a church-growth specialist."

And though that thought was totally new to me, it rang true. God had called me to invest the next chapter of my life in helping churches reach out more effectively.

That didn't mean, however, that I had the expertise my new role demanded, a point soon driven home when another church board peppered me with church-growth questions I couldn't answer. So for the next year I spent much of my time between consultations reading about ministry and church growth, listening to tapes, and asking the Holy Spirit to teach me. I began to relate what I was learning about church growth to what I already knew about architectural design. I studied church finance and was surprised to learn that the Bible clearly describes financial principles that can guide the work of the church, principles much different from those followed by the world—and most churches.

So by the time the Philadelphia church asked for my help, I realized that a facility plan intended to maximize ministry could not be created in a vacuum. It had to be developed hand in hand with a ministry plan and a financial plan. All three had to work together.

Because I had looked at the church's facility needs not in isolation but in light of ministry and finances, I had come to a conclusion that was startling, at least to me: A major building program at that time would in all likelihood stop the church's growth and create financial bondage for years to come.

Over the next ten years I went on to consult with scores of churches and learned from each of them. Because I asked facility questions from a new perspective, from the perspective of ministry and outreach, time after time I was forced to admit that some point of conventional wisdom I had embraced as an architect was untrue. Much of this conventional wisdom encouraged churches to build too big, build too soon, or build the wrong kind of building.

After thirty years of designing and encouraging churches to build new church buildings, it was painful to admit how much of my well-intentioned advice had been misguided. I could see how some churches had actually been hurt by the building programs I had helped with. Some building programs had diverted attention from meeting peoples' needs. Other churches had taken on building debts that financially crippled their ministries. In many cases the building program had slowed or stopped the growth that had prompted the new building.

These hard lessons eventually pushed me to a conclusion so unconventional that it sounds like architectural heresy: Most churches thinking of building shouldn't, at least not yet. I became convinced, in fact, that the single most valuable lesson a church can learn about building is *when not to build.* And that lesson can be summarized in three parts—three situations in which a church should not build.

   First, a church should not build if its reasons for building are wrong.

Richard Foster describes a congregational meeting his church held to pray for God's guidance concerning a proposed building program. "I went into the meeting thinking that probably we should build, and left certain that we should not," Foster writes. "The crucial turning point came when I saw the driving force behind my desiring that building to be my unarticulated feeling that a building program was the sign of a successful pastor. Theologically and philosophically, I did not believe that, but as we worshiped the Lord, the true condition of my heart was revealed. Eventually, we decided against building, a decision now validated by hindsight."[1]

Years ago a church of about 150 people in Arkansas hired me as an architect to design a new sanctuary for them. When I saw their building, I was puzzled. Though the building was older, its location was good and the congregation had never filled it.

Finally, I asked the pastor, "Why do you want a new building?"

"The first reason," he answered, "is that these people haven't done anything significant for twenty-five years. This is a way to get them to do something significant.

"Second, the people aren't giving at anywhere near the level they could or should be. A building program would motivate them to give more.

"Third, a building program will unite the people behind a common goal."

I believed he was right on all three counts and designed the new sanctuary. Now I know that this pastor was trying to do something that never works—solve nonbuilding problems with a building. That church built for the wrong reasons.

Second, a church should not build when there is a better way to meet space needs.

As I studied the Philadelphia church, I agreed at once that it had a space problem. At its rate of growth, the congregation would soon outgrow its worship space. Between Sunday school and their Christian school, their educational space was full. They had no room for additional staff offices. Building was the obvious solution, and I was tempted to lapse into my traditional architect role to produce the design.

But I couldn't. By that time I knew that was the wrong answer. "I found a room filled with missionary boxes," I told the board. "Now, those boxes don't need heat. They don't need windows or carpet, do they?" I recommended a low-cost storage and maintenance building to free up existing space for educational use.

"This barn on your property is a historic structure," I told them. "It's worth preserving. But you're not getting good use out of it." Then we discussed how they could remodel it into a gymnasium, kitchen, and educational space at half the cost of a comparable new structure.

"You can meet your need for worship space for years to come," I went on, "without the tremendous commitment of time, energy, and money involved in building a new sanctuary." The wall between the existing sanctuary and foyer could be removed to enlarge their worship area. A modest addition could provide them with a new, larger foyer, one that would make it practical to hold two Sunday morning services, thereby doubling their worship seating capacity. The new addition could also house the office space they would soon need for their growing staff.

Finally, I suggested they replace the fixed worship seating with movable seating. For the comparatively low cost of new chairs, the church could use the largest single space in the building for a wide range of activities—space that would otherwise lie useless for all but a few hours a week.

The church accepted the suggestions and completed their remodeling and modest construction projects within a couple of years. The church continued to reach out to the unchurched and within six years grew from 300 to 850.

At this church I first began to realize that of the many churches that had hired me to design new buildings, few actually needed them. Most needed to find ways to use their existing buildings more effectively. While fully using space may some-times require remodeling, refurnishing, or making modest addi-tions, in many cases it requires no money at all, only a willing-ness to do things differently. What seems obvious to me now came then as a fresh revelation: Until a church is fully using the space it has, it does not need more.

Third, a church should not build when building would increase the risk of financial bondage.

A congregation of about 175 in the Seattle area brought me in as a consultant, but only after they had put up the shell of their new building. Someone had offered the church a piece of land visible from the interstate at a bargain price. The church had jumped at it.

Confident that an attractive, highly visible building would make a strong statement to the community about the church's importance and stimulate growth, they were building a luxurious thousand-seat sanctuary. "We didn't want the inconvenience of building in phases," the pastor explained, "so we decided to build it all at once. I believe that if we just have the faith and the vision, God will provide the money."

By the time I arrived on the scene, the church, for all practical purposes, was bankrupt. All I could do was empathize with them and sadly recommend that they board up the unfinished shell, keep on using their old building, and concentrate on growth until future developments enabled them to complete their move.

The Philadelphia church faced a similar risk. When they com-missioned my study, they were still in debt for their existing building and planned to borrow most of the money for their new one. This would mean taking on loan payments larger than the congregation could meet, on the assumption that future growth would enable them to repay the loan.

Afraid this could endanger the church's growing edge, I pre-pared a detailed financial analysis that projected the potential impact of such a decision on the ministry and growth of the church. After extensive discussions the church leaders concluded such indebtedness risked not only the church's future growth but even its existing ministries. The church then adopted a plan to pay off its debt and move toward building future facilities debt free.

These three situations in which it is a mistake to build—when a church's reason for building is wrong, when there is a better way to meet space needs, and when building would risk financial bondage—suggest three positive principles. These principles can guide churches in determining whether it is time to build (the time to build *does* come) and what to do instead when building is premature.

1. *The Principle of Focus.* A church should build only when it can do so without shifting its focus from ministering to people to building a building.

2. *The Principle of Use.* A church needs more space only when it is fully using the space it already has.

3. *The Principle of Provision.* A church should build only when it can do so within the income God has provided and without using funds needed for the church's present and future ministries to people.

These three principles, which the following chapters explain and illustrate, have for more than a decade guided my work with growing churches. Each year I see more evidence of their power to unleash the church to do its real work. They have enabled congregations to leave behind limiting ways of thinking about, using, and paying for church buildings in favor of ways that free up most of the time, money, and energy traditionally invested in buildings. These resources can then be redirected to the true mission of the church: ministering to the needs of people in Christ's name.

It can happen in your church, too.

The Principle of Focus

A church should build
only when it can do so
without shifting its focus
from ministering to people
to building a building.

2

Can Buildings Kill Church Growth?

After organizing with forty-eight members in 1947, Champlain Church[1] grew within four years to 116 members, pushing the limits of its rented facility. To have room for continuous growth the church took the next logical step. They built. But then a surprising thing happened. Immediately, Champlain Church stopped growing. Membership hovered between 90 and 115 until finally, twenty-three years later, the church's membership loss was restored. As the chart shows, it was not until 1980, twenty-nine years after the building program, that the growth of the church resumed.

While conventional wisdom says that church buildings create growth, the experience of Champlain Church is actually more common: Church buildings often kill church growth. In over forty years as a church architect and consultant, I have seen it happen time and again. An exciting, growing congregation builds to make room for continued growth, only to see their growth stop as soon as they build.

FIGURE 1

Growth at the Champlain Church

Now, I'm not against church buildings. After all, I am an architect. I have designed buildings for churches most of my life. There is a right time and a right way to build. But in far too many cases building programs have killed, or at least slowed, the growth of vital congregations. Why?

A major reason is that the church's focus changes. Most church growth occurs because a church effectively ministers to people's needs. Its focus is on people. But often, when a growing church builds, its focus shifts from people to building. That change of focus kills church growth.

Take, for example, Grace Community Church, a suburban congregation in a large Midwest metropolitan area. In the seventies their attendance grew from 200 to 1500. During this period they built a 1000-seat worship space that corresponded to their needs and resources but did not interrupt their growth. But before this building was paid for, the congregation decided to build again so they wouldn't have to keep holding double services on Sunday morning. They built a 4000-seat worship area and have had little growth since.

For years now the people of Grace Community have worshiped in a space more than half empty. In more than a decade, seldom has a Sunday passed when the pastor has not appealed for funds to pay the mortgage. One member who normally would have invited his friends to church told me, "I'd be embarrassed to invite any of my friends to our church, because they'd think the only reason I invited them was to get them to help pay the debt."

Recently I visited with a wonderful retired couple from that congregation. I knew something of the years of devoted service they had given the church, often behind the scenes. "We feel so privileged to have been a part of the ministry of the church," they told me. Then they went on to describe how they had been able to generously support the church's building programs.

Though I didn't tell them, I was saddened by what they said. They had given their lives in loving service to God and others, yet they measured their servanthood not by the many lives they had touched with God's love but by dollars given to building programs. After years of hearing their pastor appeal for money for buildings, they, and doubtless many others in the congregation, had come to view the building itself as the work of the church. While the church had continued to serve its members, the major focus of the church had become paying for the building. That change of focus had helped kill the church's growth.

At Grace Community the change of focus came about primarily through too much debt, but that's not the only way it can happen. A church of 200 in New York had outgrown both its worship and educational space. They asked me to develop a facilities plan that would give them room to keep growing. After studying their situation, I proposed a combination of remodeling and utilization changes that would require little or no indebtedness yet provide the space they needed.

But I cautioned the pastor on one point. "Paul," I said, "I know you have people in this congregation who have the skills to do this remodeling themselves. Because you want to keep putting your funds into the ministries that have been so effective, it will be tempting to let your people do the remodeling. Don't let them. Hire someone to do it for you. Otherwise, the time and energy your people now put into caring for the homeless, for runaways, for other displaced people, will be diverted to the building. It will change your church's focus, and your ministry will suffer."

The church adopted my recommendations on every point but one: The people decided to do the remodeling themselves. Two years later I had lunch with that pastor. "Ray," he said, "you were right. We did the remodeling ourselves, and it changed our focus."

Three years later the church had begun to grow again, but it still had not recovered its lost momentum. The change of focus had crippled the church's ministry and interrupted its growth.

A building program can change a church's focus even before construction begins. An established urban congregation of 300 built a multipurpose building used for worship on Sunday and as a gymnasium and for a host of other events during the week. They regarded this gymnasium as a temporary building to be replaced as soon as possible by a "real sanctuary." During the next six years the church grew to 700. At that point the church's leaders spent three years planning and raising funds for a major building program. During those three years, the church's growth slowed almost to zero. Why?

Unlike Grace Community, the problem was not indebtedness. While the building would stretch the church financially, the leaders were careful not to commit so much to the building that it would endanger the staffing and funding of ministry programs.

And unlike the New York congregation, the problem was not that the people did the actual construction themselves. Rather, the church's leaders put so much time and energy into planning the building and raising funds that it changed the church's focus.

The truth is, the church already had plenty of room to grow. By adding a third worship service and adding Christian education classes at nontraditional times, the church could have grown to 1400 or 1500 in their existing building. Instead, the church decided to build, diverting the leaders' best creative energy to the building program even before the building began.

This changed focus was also evident among the members. When asked how the church was doing, members usually told how the building program was going and often expressed impatience with the process. They honestly believed the church could not move ahead until the new building was finished. The building program, rather than motivating members to reach out, tended to put the church's ministries on hold.

By the time this church completes its building, the creative ministry that produced the church's most rapid growth will be five or six years in the past. After so many years of focusing on building, nothing short of a miracle will be able to quickly return the church's focus to ministering to people's needs.

Far more likely is that upon completion of their building the church will feel it has arrived. If their response is typical, they will not say it in so many words, but the members' actions will say, "We have accomplished the Lord's work." They will sit back and wait for the church to grow.

Many members will probably think that the church is growing even if it is not. Why? Because the new building itself—the enlargement of the physical plant—will create the illusion of growth. For yet one more church, building a building will have become an unfortunate substitute for the church's real work.

Planning a building, constructing a building, paying for a building—any of these can become substitutes for ministry, though no church would ever set out to make that happen. Whenever building is allowed to become a church's focus, even temporarily, the church's ministries suffer, and growth slows or stops.

Building, however, does not have to hurt the church. A church can keep its focus on ministry, even through planning, constructing, and paying for a building. The first step in making that happen is for the congregation and its leaders, even before they enter the planning phase of building, to commit themselves to the principle of focus: *Our church will build only when we can do so without changing our focus from ministry to building.*

In 1981 a couple went to a small community on Cape Cod to start a church. While the pastor worked as a plumber to support his family, he and his family began to invite their non-Christian neighbors to a Bible study in their home. Before long they had to add a second Bible study.

Within a couple of years the church grew to about fifty adults, who worshiped in the Odd Fellows Lodge building, and about thirty children who met in the Masonic Lodge up the street. The church needed more space, and there was no larger space in town they could rent. So they bought land and asked me to help with building plans.

After studying their situation, I was convinced that a building program at that time would stop the church's growth. I recommended that the church set a goal of growing to 150 before building. My experience had taught me that a church needs fifty giving units—150 to 200 people—before it is financially strong enough to build without handicapping its ministry.

Still, the church had to have more space right away. To meet that need, I recommended two changes. First, the church should go to double services. Second, the basement of the Odd Fellows building was lying unused, and in its existing form it was unusable. I suggested that the church offer to remodel and redecorate the basement at church expense in exchange for the owners' permission to use the space.

I also suggested three financial goals for the church. First, pay off the remaining $20,000 debt on the parsonage as soon as possible. Second, pay off the mortgage on the building site. Third, accumulate as large a building fund as possible before building.

The church continued to grow, enduring tremendous inconveniences and frustrations because they met in a building barely adequate for their needs. The temptation to build before they were financially ready must have been tremendous. Yet the people persevered, making do with rented facilities until they could build without endangering salaries and ministries.

After five years, the church had reached all three of the financial goals necessary to enable them to build. They had grown to 150, paid off the parsonage and land, and accumulated a substantial building fund. By this time they had absolutely no more room to grow. It was time to build.

When the church broke ground in 1988, the pastor knew the building program would not jeopardize the church's ministries.

Yes, building can kill a church's growth, but it doesn't have to. A growing church *can* plan and pay for a building program in such a way that the members never take their focus off meeting the needs of people. The way to accomplish this is neither difficult nor mysterious, as the following chapters show. It just calls for a bit of unconventional wisdom.

3

The Myth of Sacred Space

It was an architect's dream come true. First Church had the money to do it right. The building committee gave me the freedom to incorporate into the design everything I believed a sanctuary should be. This was the opportunity I'd been waiting for—the chance to design the ultimate sanctuary.

I didn't have to think twice to know what I wanted to capture in that sanctuary's design. Years of architectural training, many more years of practical experience specializing in church architecture, and my own love for the beauty of the great historic sanctuaries—all these had prepared me for this moment. I was ready.

I told the building committee what I had told dozens of building committees before: "The sanctuary is the heart of the church, a sacred space devoted exclusively to the worship of God. Building your sanctuary should take priority over all the church's building needs. Until you have such a sanctuary, the church's worship will never be all it should be."

The committee enthusiastically supported my proposal, and I set out to design the sanctuary of my dreams. The building I would design would make people want to attend First Church. Once they were there, the environment would speak to their spirits. The stained glass, the pipe organ, the strong vertical lines, the dynamic symmetry—more than mere aesthetics, these design elements would draw people to God, inspire them to worship. And through worship they would be changed. No mere bricks and mortar, this building. No, it would be a means of grace.

My confidence in the power of architecture was hardly unusual. During my architectural training I had been taught, as most architects are, that the key to solving social problems was to create new and better environments in which to live, work, learn, and, in my case, to worship. Though I would not discover it for several years, there was a problem with that belief: It was wrong.

That realization came gradually. A church in Nampa, Idaho, asked me to design a worship space for them with a multilevel platform, movable choir seats, portable risers, and ramps to make it easy to move props and equipment on and off stage. They envisioned using the space for dramas at Christmas and Easter, for a symphony orchestra, for big or small choirs that could be moved to various locations. With the experience of designing that sanctuary, cracks began to appear in my traditional thinking.

Three years later I designed my first totally flexible church facility. Worship, Sunday school, fellowship, and recreation all took place in the same area. The building had no "sacred space"—space set aside exclusively for worship. Though the congregation saw this building as temporary, to be replaced later by a single-use sanctuary, in designing that building I became a bit more open to new possibilities.

My traditional thinking was further challenged when I left my architectural firm to become a consultant. Because I wanted to help churches do facility planning in a biblical context, I spent a lot of time studying the New Testament. What I found startled me.

First, I discovered that sanctuary is an Old Testament concept that was abolished in Christ. Sanctuary means "where God dwells," and in the Old Testament the Holy of Holies was indeed a special dwelling place for God. But when Jesus breathed his last on the cross, the curtain of the temple tore from top to bottom and opened the Holy of Holies—where God dwelled—to all humanity.

Scripture leaves no doubt about where God dwelled from that moment on:

"God doesn't live in temples made by human hands" (Acts 17:24).

[God] doesn't live in man-made temples" (Acts 17:24).

"Don't you realize that all of you together are the house of God, and that the Spirit of God lives among you in his house?" (1 Cor. 3:16).

"Your body is the home of the Holy Spirit" (1 Cor. 6:19).

"What a foundation you stand on now: the apostles and prophets, and the cornerstone of the building is Jesus Christ himself! We who believe are carefully joined together with Christ as parts of a beautiful, constantly growing temple for God" (Eph. 2:20-21).

"And now you have become living building-stones for God's use in building his house" (1 Peter 2:5).

All my life I had heard that the church building, especially the sanctuary, was "God's house." Had I lived before Christ's earthly ministry, it might have been appropriate to give that kind of reverence to the temple. But my Bible study now convinced me that my thinking was two thousand years out of date. As Jesus explained to the woman at the well, "It's not *where* we worship that counts, but *how* we worship" (John 4:21).

For the first time I realized no human could ever design a sanctuary. No amount of money, no amount of stained glass and carpet and padded pews could transform bricks and mortar into the dwelling place of God. God has already chosen his dwelling place, and he has chosen not "temples made with hands" but the hearts of his people.

Second, my Bible study showed me that the New Testament church owned no church buildings, though they held both large-group and small-group meetings. The large-group gatherings, for the most part, were not meetings of the church—believers—but rather meetings for public evangelism, something like today's evangelistic crusades. Such public evangelism took place in the temple courts, in a public market, in synagogues, in a rented hall, on a riverbank. It seems never to have crossed the apostles' minds that they might need to build large auditoriums to conduct public evangelism. Meeting space already existed, and besides, these evangelistic crusades were not ongoing year-round meetings but rather part of the church-planting process. Once a church was established, the large evangelistic meetings were succeeded by a network of house churches in which the believers worshiped together and ministered to one another.

In Jerusalem people came to Christ by the tens of thousands and possibly hundreds of thousands. In our day sucn rapid growth would promptly run into obstacles. Where could we find facilities large enough for all those people to meet? Even the temple courts would have been overrun quickly had they all tried to meet together. But meeting space was no problem for those first Christians, because as more people became Christians, more homes—thousands of them—became available as meeting places.

The first-century church prayed, taught, evangelized, healed, baptized, ate together, celebrated the Lord's Supper, shared to meet the needs of others, sang, worshiped, and praised God. And they did it all without owning a single church building.

For almost three centuries the church built few if any buildings, and it continued to enjoy the most vigorous period of ministry and growth the church has ever known. Then disaster struck. Constantine declared Christianity the state religion. The church became less and less a community of believers, more and more a religious institution. The church built buildings and more buildings. Its focus had shifted. The church's most dynamic era had come to an end.

Now, I know the gospel is supposed to be good news, but for an architect, especially for an architect who had already invested most of a lifetime in designing church buildings, my biblical findings did not much feel like good news. I found it hard to admit my mistakes, to concede that much of my life's work had been misguided. Had my decades of service to the church as an architect been wasted? Even more important, were my training and experience of any further use to the church? Or was the whole idea of a "church architect" inconsistent with a New Testament vision of church, a church without sanctuaries?

In time I found comfort in this thought: The church needs buildings. Whether borrowed, rented, shared, leased, built, or bought, the church will always need buildings. What would happen, I wondered, if I left behind my arrogant belief that I could design a building that would somehow draw people to God, cause them to worship, inspire them to change? What if I started with the idea that the church is people, and its mission is to meet the needs of people in Christ's name? What kind of building would result?

To find an answer I looked to the words of Christ. I noticed that he continually described himself and his kingdom with words such as *meek, lowly, kind, merciful, good, just,* and *humble.* What kind of design, I wondered, would reflect these values?

Personally, I loved Gothic architecture with its ornate grandeur, but it clearly did not reflect the values of Jesus. Rather, it was a monument to the pride and power of humanity. A design based on Jesus' values would not be ornate but simple; it would not be pretentious but restrained. The space would not overpower people with its lavishness or size, but make them feel welcome and comfortable. The very style of the architecture would say that people are more important than the building itself.

I also looked around at growing churches for clues. Most growing churches, I found, used their buildings differently than did nongrowing churches. For example, they held multiple worship services and Sunday schools. They had learned that they could not build big enough to continue a single service and still keep their growing edge. They used space for multiple purposes throughout the week—Christian education, fellowship, recreation.

Churches with consistent growth were churches determined to keep their focus on people. To keep that focus, they had left behind some traditional ways of thinking about and using their facilities. As a result, facilities demanded less of their members' time, money, and energy, and those resources were available for meeting people's needs.

I came to see that unbiblical attitudes toward church buildings were among the greatest barriers to ministry and church growth in our time. In contrast to the first-century church that ministered powerfully and grew rapidly without owning buildings, most churches today think they cannot minister or grow without buildings. In contrast to that first-century church that worshiped on the first day of the week in the same space where families lived the other six and a half days, many churches today worship in single-use space that lies unused 160 hours or more a week. This setting apart of "sacred space" for worship only, intended as an expression of reverence, actually hinders the work of God. It shifts the focus of the church as members divert time, money, and energy away from ministering to people so they can build and pay for unnecessary buildings.

After what I had learned I could no longer champion the sanctuary—space designed for worship only. I began to recommend instead what I call a "ministry center," a large area with a level floor and movable furnishings that can be used not only for corporate worship but also for a host of other ministry activities throughout the week. In short, I quit viewing church buildings as sacred space and started seeing them, and designing them, as tools for ministry.

If the church's mission is to minister to people in Christ's name, church buildings can have only one legitimate function: to serve as tools to help church members better fulfill that mission. We can no longer afford to spend hundreds of thousands of dollars on "sacred" but unnecessary buildings that lie vacant 80 or 90 percent of the time. If our focus is truly on people rather than buildings, that reality will shape the kinds of buildings we design, how we use them, how much we spend on them, and how much time, energy, and money we keep free for the real work of the church: meeting people's needs.

4

Three Things Church Buildings Can Never Do

If you had eavesdropped on a phone conversation in my office some years ago, you might have heard something like this:

"I'd like you to come talk to my board about a new building," the pastor said.

"That sounds good," I answered. "What do you need?"

"The people need a challenge. They haven't done anything for years, and a building program will wake them up and unite them behind a cause."

"You're right," I said. "Nothing is more exciting than building."

"There's a lot of money in our church," the pastor went on, "but giving has been going downhill lately. A new building will increase stewardship. If we plan a project for a million dollars, I think that will be enough to really challenge the people. I've decided to hire a professional fundraiser to raise about a third of that amount through a three-year giving drive. We can borrow the rest."

"Will your regular income cover the payments?" I wanted to know.

"Not yet, but the new building should bring in new people, and the increased giving will cover the payments."

"That's exciting! With that kind of money we can design an award-winning structure that will put your church on the map, one the people of your community will want to attend. What kind of building do you need?"

"Well, we haven't grown for years, so our sanctuary is old and should make a good family life center. That should attract families. So I guess it's logical to build a new sanctuary."

"How many should we plan for?"

"We have around three hundred regular attenders, so we should plan for real growth—say eight hundred to a thousand."

"That should really give your people a vision of the possibilities and motivate them to reach out. When can we start?"

Though I'm not proud of it, I've had many conversations much like this one, and passed along the same conventional wisdom I'd heard about building programs from countless pastors and church leaders. I now realize that the "conventional wisdom" includes many fallacies. When a church depends on these fallacies, disappointment and sometimes disaster result. Here are three of the most common and costly of the false expectations I am guilty of having promoted.

False Expectation 1
Building will stimulate growth

When I designed my dream sanctuary for First Church (chapter 3), I fully expected the building to attract new people, to increase the church's rate of growth. It was the most architecturally perfect building I had ever designed. The congregation was united behind the building program, there were no financial problems—nothing in the process to hinder growth. If ever one of my buildings was going to create growth, this one would.

Several years after the building was complete, I charted the church's growth history. Before the building program the church had been growing at a steady rate of 3 percent a year. After the building program, the church had grown at 3 percent a year.

It was humbling for this architect to finally admit that no church building, however perfectly designed, can make a church grow. The most a building can do is *allow* a church to grow.

In one church of 160, those who "wanted the church to grow" were promoting a plan to relocate to a business district centrally located among the communities the church served. Relocation, they claimed, would make the church grow. "Our church is in an out-of-the-way place," they said. "Our building is full. The basement smells bad and there's nothing we can do about it. And we don't have enough parking."

Actually, none of that was true. They could double parking capacity simply by paving and marking the parking lot. All the basement needed was a good ventilation system. With creative planning, their building would give the congregation room to double before it needed to build. And their location was actually better than the one proposed for a new building.

It's true that unattractive or inadequate facilities can hinder growth, but in this case church facilities were not the problem; they were an excuse. The real problem was that the church was doing absolutely nothing to grow. They didn't advertise, they didn't have a yellow pages listing, they didn't even follow up on visitors.

Their attitude toward outreach was symbolized by two stern, silent old men who stood guard at the door. Though each wore a "Greeter" badge, they looked more like people you might recruit to frighten children at a Halloween haunted house. When I visited their service, it was not until I greeted the "greeters" that either spoke to me. Though this congregation did not need a new building, some members preferred to promote a building program rather than do the work of outreach that really would bring growth.

False Expectation 2
Building will improve members' giving to ministry

The myth that building programs will motivate more giving to ministry is an especially dangerous one, because it often appears to be true. Building programs usually do motivate people to give. Especially at the outset, large sums of money can be raised for a building program. Some members may even increase their giving for the duration of a long-term mortgage. So what's wrong with expecting a building program to increase giving to ministry?

The problem is that building buildings is not the same as ministry. Building buildings is not the work of the church. The work of the church is to meet people's needs. While a building program may motivate people to give more to pay for buildings, seldom is the increased giving enough to cover the cost of the building.

A rapidly growing church in Oklahoma earmarked 5 percent of all its income for local outreach. These funds were invested in various local ministries in which members of the church were involved, including an inner city ministry, a ministry to pregnant teens, and several other ongoing projects.

When the congregation launched a multimillion dollar building program, the people gave generously in response. However, when building costs exceeded estimates, the church began looking for places to cut expenses. They abandoned their earmarking of 5 percent of income for local outreach and redirected most of those funds to the building program. While total giving increased, funds directed to meeting the needs of people decreased.

This church's experience tends to be the rule, not the exception. While building may temporarily increase giving, it usually results in less, not more, money available for ministry.

False Expectation 3
Building will motivate people to minister

One of the first churches I worked for as an architect was a congregation of fifty in a small Kansas town. The moment I saw their building I understood why they wanted to build. It was small, dark, and dilapidated. The members were embarrassed to invite their friends. I would have been embarrassed, too. If only they had a new, attractive building, the leaders thought, the people would no longer be embarrassed and would reach out to the community.

I helped them design a building that gave them room to grow. It had a bright nursery, attractive Sunday school rooms, and plenty of parking. They built that building and opened the doors.

That was thirty-five years ago. Though the church has grown some, today it still has not outgrown that building. Why? After all, they did a lot of things right. They really did need a building, the building they built was appropriate to the congregation's needs, and the cost of the building was reasonable.

This church's mistake was that they expected a building to motivate people to minister. If during the building program church leaders had established an outreach plan and recruited and trained people so they would be ready to reach out once the building was complete, no doubt the church would have grown.

These three false expectations all have one thing in common: They all assume that buildings can meet nonbuilding needs. To expect church buildings to stimulate growth, inspire healthy stewardship, or motivate outreach is to expect church buildings to do the impossible. Why? Because these are all ministry needs, not building needs, and buildings cannot minister.

If buildings cannot minister, what purpose do they serve? They are *tools for ministry.* A wrench can't repair a faucet, and a word processor can't write a book, but they can help the plumber and the writer do their jobs better. In the same way, an appropriate building—whether borrowed, rented, or owned—

can provide space well suited to the ministries it serves. It can help people feel more comfortable and welcome. It can provide workspace and equipment to increase efficiency. It can make the ministries of the church more accessible to the community. It can do all these and more.

But one thing a building can never do: It can never minister. Only people can do that.

The Motivation Test

Why Do You Want to Build?

Which of the following reasons to build are motivating your church's leaders to consider building? Check those that apply.

_____ 1. A new building will attract new people to the church.

_____ 2. Members will be more motivated to reach out to others once we have a new building.

_____ 3. Our new building will inspire people to worship.

_____ 4. A building program will involve more people in the work of the church.

_____ 5. A building program will motivate our people to give more generously to the work of the church.

_____ 6. A building program will unify our people behind a significant challenge.

_____ 7. A new building will make a statement to the community about our church's importance.

_____ 8. Our people will take greater pride in their church when the new building is complete.

_____ 9. A new facility will provide our people with a more effective tool for ministry.

Interpreting Your Answers

All nine of these reasons for building are common, but most are not adequate reasons to build. Statements 1 through 3 express the expectation that the building will minister. To attract new people to the church, motivate members to reach out, and inspire worship are all important goals for the church, but they are all ministry goals. Buildings don't minister; people do. No building can meet these nonbuilding needs.

Statements 4 through 6 are based on the assumption that building buildings is the work of the church, or at least an integral part of the church's work; therefore, when people unite behind a building program by giving their time, money, or energy to it, they are doing the work of the church. However, this common attitude is simply unbiblical. Building buildings is not the work of the church; the church's work is to minister to people in Christ's name. When a church builds for any of these three reasons, building buildings has become an unfortunate substitute for the real work of the church.

Statements 7 and 8 express worldly values that often creep into the church without our noticing. The notion that "bigger and better" buildings are symbols of prestige or success is unworthy of a church that is called to reject materialism and be a servant people.

Statement 9, building to provide church members with a more effective tool for ministry, is the only motivation for building consistent with the church's purpose. If the church regards buildings as tools and nothing more, not only will this affect the decision *whether* you build, but *how* to build. A building designed to serve will look much different from one designed to impress.

If you checked any of the first eight statements, your church needs to further clarify its motives for building before it moves ahead. To fail to do so will almost certainly bring disappointing results.

If you checked only statement 9, congratulations! You have passed the motivation test. But that does not necessarily mean you should build. You also need to determine whether a major building program is the best way to meet your space needs and whether your church is financially ready to build. The next two sections of the book will help you answer those questions.

The Principle of Use

A church needs more space
only when it is fully using
the space it already has.

5

Seven Ways to Avoid Costly Building Mistakes

"You can see our problem," the pastor said, motioning toward the empty pews. "This auditorium seats 400; we seldom hit 150. Sunday mornings this place feels almost as empty as it does right now. Our little group rattling around in here week after week gets to be depressing. I'm convinced it's keeping us from growing. We'd like you to recommend a way to remodel this sanctuary to make it smaller, warmer, more comfortable. Then maybe we can grow."

How had this situation come about? Twenty years earlier the leaders of this Oklahoma City church had said, "If we build a big sanctuary, people will come to fill it." They had built the building, but the people had not come.

I could have drawn up plans for corrective remodeling, but the church, still saddled with debt from that earlier building, could not afford it. Because they expected the building to generate growth, they had built too big too soon.

Another church in New York state faced the opposite problem. Innovative ministries to teens and young adults had attracted new people. Every Sunday saw double worship services and Sunday school, with classes spilling over into a house, the parsonage, and the restaurant next door. Their full-to-overflowing buildings testified to the excitement of belonging to this church family.

But their growth had bumped against the limits of their space. With no more room, growth had stopped. Not only were they crowded, but one building—the one the teens used—was leaky, poorly heated, and structurally unsafe. This church faced the problem of too little too late.

Building too big too soon and building too little too late are both costly mistakes, but both can be avoided. In my consulting work I recommend that churches follow seven steps to plan their buildings wisely.

1. Know your community

A church in a bedroom community near San Francisco was considering whether to build. When I asked what future ministries they envisioned, they mentioned, among other things, a ministry for the poor, perhaps a soup kitchen or clothing closet. But when the pastor checked the local demographics, he found that almost no poor families lived in the neighborhood. Instead, the church's neighborhood attracted upper-income families. His people, this pastor realized, were fantasizing about ministry to a group not even present in their community.

The pastor believed that to reach their neighborhood they needed a building appropriate to their changing surroundings. Their older, poorly maintained facility with an amateurish sign tacked to its side hardly looked inviting to their upwardly mobile neighbors. I suspected the pastor was right when, as I spoke to the congregation, mice scampered across the platform and ran beneath the pews in front of me.

This congregation awoke to what they needed to do and did it. The last I heard they were getting ready for a neighborhood get-acquainted party to introduce themselves to their "future members." For the occasion they planned to raise a big, brightly colored tent on the site where their new building would soon appear.

Before your church can tailor its ministries and facilities to those it hopes to reach, you must first get to know the needs of your community.

2. Evaluate current and long-term needs

To find out how well current facilities serve a church's ministries, I recommend an effectiveness review. Write down on the floor plan of your building what happens in each room during the various hours of the week. Then identify anything needed to improve each ministry's effectiveness. Does it need new leadership? Additional training or support for leaders? More money?

Since facilities often are blamed for nonfacility needs, it is important to identify nonfacility needs first. For example, to try to revitalize the church's ministry to teens by building or remodeling a meeting space is pointless if the fundamental problem with that ministry is unqualified leadership.

Once nonfacility needs have been separated from facility needs, the next step is to create an itemized list of space needs, both immediate and long-term. For each ministry, include how much space is needed and what kind of facility would work best.

Sometimes defining facility needs involves more than determining the amount and kind of space needed. A church near New York City had a major ministry to the poor, the homeless, and runaway teens. Even with two services they had outgrown their sanctuary, so they bought land to build. On further reflection, though, they realized that relocation would separate them from the very people to whom they ministered. While they needed more space, the *location* of that space was critical. They sold the new land and used the money to remodel their worship space. By fully using space in two adjacent houses and a commercial building they were able to expand in the same location.

The process of itemizing current and long-term facility needs is valuable to any church. For the church that considers major remodeling or new construction, this step must be completed before an architect can draw up appropriate plans. For churches that consider building and for those that do not, this process lays the groundwork for using present space more effectively. (For step-by-step instructions for writing a program of needs, see the appendix.)

3. Use present facilities to the maximum

Once a church has clearly defined its space needs, it is ready to find ways to meet those needs. That search should always begin at the same place: the church's present buildings. Churches that think they are running out of room often are surprised to learn that they can double or triple in size without a major building program simply by changing how they think about and use their present space. Until a church fully utilizes its existing building, a need for more space does not exist. Following are some ways to solve space problems without new facilities.

Move groups to the right size rooms. Many churches have at least one little class in a big room and one big class in a little room.

Change the group size to fit the room. When a group outgrows its room, sometimes it works to divide the class. If a church has small classes in big rooms, a teaching method that combines classes may solve the problem. Large-group team teaching may make better use of space *and* improve learning. Some children's classes can grow in the same room with the addition of an assistant teacher or workers.

Change furniture. You can increase worship seating as much as 20 percent by replacing pews with individual seating. If that seating is movable, the space also becomes available for multiple use.

A room that uses appropriate tables and chairs can hold twice as many people as one filled with overstuffed furniture. For preschool or kindergarten classes, the solution may be to get rid of the furniture and have the children sit on a carpeted floor for their activities. Oversize play equipment—such as a slide—may waste space. If full-size cribs are eating up needed nursery space, replace them with half-size or stacked cribs.

Find new uses for any space not already fully used. One of the first places to look is the worship area. A church in western Pennsylvania with excess worship seating removed several back rows and installed room dividers, carving out needed space for a foyer, a fellowship area, and a Sunday school class.

A foyer can be ideal for receptions, board meetings, or Sunday school class dinners. Some churches use folding walls to divide large foyers for Sunday school space, then open them back up before people arrive for worship. The foyer of one church in Kansas City doubles as an office reception area; along one wall—in space not otherwise used—they've installed six staff and secretarial modules.

Consider what minor remodeling can do. Can you increase usable space by taking a wall out? Putting a wall in? Installing a folding wall across part of the foyer? Enclosing a hallway with a folding wall?

Build or rent a storage building. If you now use potential meeting rooms for storage, this is an inexpensive way to free up space in a hurry.

Use creative scheduling. A children's ministry brought in scores of children from the community. Because they met on Saturday, they could use the only space big enough to hold the group: the worship area.

In addition to multiple Sunday services and Sunday school sessions, how about an additional worship service on a weeknight? One church has a Monday evening "Sunday school." Not only is this good stewardship, it also ministers to those who can't come on Sundays.

4. Use alternate space

Almost every community has meeting space churches may use, often just for the asking: homes, motel party rooms, schools, lodge halls, community rooms in banks or apartment complexes. Young-singles classes often work better in restaurants than in church buildings. Some people who are uncomfortable coming to a church building will gladly participate in groups that meet elsewhere.

5. Consider a modest addition

A Massachusetts congregation started holding double worship services, but a lot of people were unhappy with the arrangement because they couldn't visit with friends who attended the other service. Recognizing the importance of such fellowship, the church made two changes. First, they extended the period between services to thirty minutes to give worshipers leaving the first service time to visit with those arriving for the second; and, second, they built a larger foyer to provide a place to visit. While neither change by itself would have done the job, providing both time and space for fellowship solved the problem.

A modest addition may also be called for when multiple staff work in a building originally designed with office space for only one pastor. When professional and support staff offices are scattered, teamwork suffers and the staff is less accessible to the public. While some congregations can create a centralized administrative complex by remodeling, others will need to consider an addition.

6. Repair and redecorate

A church building should feel warm, pleasant, and comfortable. In a word, it should look loved. When a new pastor came to a church in upstate New York, he found a badly neglected building. Years before, the congregation had realized they needed to relocate and bought land elsewhere. They then quit spending money to maintain their old building. Partly because of the unloved appearance of the church building the congregation had quit growing. But until the congregation grew, it would not be able to afford to build.

This pastor, then, was able to challenge the people to repair and redecorate their old building as a necessary step toward resuming their growth. They cleaned out junk, replaced outdated signs on classroom doors, put new furniture in the nursery, and fixed the plumbing. Once again, their building looks loved. It no longer stands in the way of growth.

7. Seek creative parking solutions

When one church needed more parking, a doctor in the church offered the parking lot at his clinic two blocks away. The church leaders agreed to park there to free parking space at the church.

A church near Philadelphia uses stacked parking. Members volunteer to park bumper-to-bumper at the back of the lot and wait patiently when it's time to go home. This leaves the most convenient parking for visitors.

Can you use the school parking lot across the street? The shopping center down the block? Could you create a "park and ride" center a half mile away, with the church providing a shuttle bus? Most parking problems, however stubborn they may at first appear, have solutions.

While all these solutions to parking problems have been used successfully, several of them also create inconvenience for church members. It's the same with some of the other suggested space solutions such as multiple use of space, movable furnishings, use of off-campus meeting space, and meeting at nontraditional times. I've discovered that a distinguishing mark of practically every growing church is that the people of the church are willing to be inconvenienced for the work of the church. When church members will not volunteer for some inconveniences, the church is unlikely to grow.

Solomon wrote: "Any enterprise is built by wise planning, becomes strong through common sense, and profits wonderfully by keeping abreast of the facts" (Prov. 24:3-4). The seven suggestions are no magic formula. They simply represent wise planning, common sense, and a way to keep abreast of the facts. Churches that apply them can avoid the most common and costly building mistakes.

A church that keeps current on steps 1 and 2 will not be taken by surprise when it needs to build. A church that makes full use of its present space (steps 3 through 7) will not rush into an unnecessary building program.

By following these seven suggestions, a church can avoid either building too little too late or too big too soon, and can instead build just the right building at just the right time.

6

Remodeling for Growth

Every year thousands of congregations build new buildings when they could have met their space needs equally well through remodeling, and for a fraction of the cost in time, money, and energy. Not only is remodeling often more economical, it also preserves. When we remodel, we use what we have, which has an impact on the whole chain of environmental preservation and sets a positive example in our communities to avoid waste and preserve creation.

While remodeling often offers the best solution to a church's space needs, the process can also be complicated by many possible pitfalls, some unique to remodeling. The following case study illustrates how a congregation can use a planning process much like the one outlined in chapter 5 to shape a major program of remodeling.

When the director of children's ministries at First Christian Church in Columbus, Indiana, proposed removing the walls around two small rooms to create a large, open nursery area, she ran into resistance. Though the building was fifty years old, no wall had ever been removed.

The reason was easy to understand. When the congregation decided to build in the late 1930s, they interviewed two of the most prominent architects in the country—Frank Lloyd Wright and Eliel Saarinen. The building committee commissioned Eliel Saarinen to design a building of a new style, "not a dead style of an alien culture" but one consistent with the contemporary culture of the community. The result was a building famous for its innovative design, years ahead of its time. None of the local church leaders dared trust their own judgment when it came to tinkering with the work of an architectural great.

This children's director was faced with the most basic of tensions in remodeling: the need to simultaneously change and preserve—to update the building to serve the needs of a growing congregation and changing community and at the same time preserve the architectural integrity of the original design. To address these concerns she prepared a carefully researched proposal and presented it to the church leadership who then authorized the proposed remodeling.

The leaders of First Christian Church recognized, however, that in knocking out a couple of walls they had barely scratched the surface. They were expecting growth, planning for growth, making major changes in leadership roles within the congregation specifically to stimulate growth. But their facility was not ready to handle growth. To find a way to correct this, the church created a long-range facility-planning committee. While no two churches can follow the same remodeling plan, the basic *process* of planning for remodeling is the same for any church, whether large or small, whether the existing building is a historic landmark or an architectural embarrassment.

Here, then, using the experience of First Christian to illustrate, are five steps your church can take to develop and implement a master remodeling plan uniquely suited to your congregation's needs.

1. Identify maintenance and modernization needs

Fire and safety codes have changed since your facility was built. Has your building kept pace with those changes? Is your building accessible to the physically handicapped? Do you have an adequate security system? What is the condition of the basic systems of the building—electrical wiring, plumbing, heating/ventilation/air conditioning? Are these systems cost effective? How much longer can they last?

Is your building properly insulated to meet current energy conservation requirements? Have any structural problems appeared? Does the building leak moisture through the roof or walls? To survey these needs you may need professional assistance.

While First Christian's building complied with all safety codes when it was built, today's codes require more fire-safe exits and panic hardware on exterior doors. Making the building accessible to the handicapped will mean building a ramp to the first floor, adding an elevator that connects all three floors, and installing toilet facilities to meet their needs.

The building has no security system but needs one. The electrical wiring met codes when it was built, but today the main service panel is so antiquated it can't even be worked on. The heating, ventilation, and air conditioning system is no longer cost efficient and needs to be totally replaced. First Christian faces major expenses in bringing its existing facility up to present building standards.

It may not be all that exciting to spend money, or raise money, for something as unglamorous as replacing electrical wiring, but all these maintenance and modernization needs belong in your master remodeling plan.

2. Determine space needs

The next step is to figure out the short- and long-term space needs for all the church's ministries. Do you have enough worship seating for your present needs? For five years from now? Do you have enough educational space? Is it the right kind of space for your needs? Do you have an adequate fellowship area? Does your administrative area allow all your staff to work together? Does your church have ministries with special facilities needs such as a counseling center, a preschool, recreation, or outreach programs? What are the short- and long-term facility needs of each of these ministries? (For a detailed guide to writing such a program of needs, see the appendix.)

While some churches will need to remodel worship space, that's not a problem for First Christian. So well did Saarinen design the worship area that fifty years later it requires nothing more than routine maintenance. What *is* a problem is that two services are held in a space designed for one. For traffic to flow smoothly between multiple services, a large foyer/fellowship space is needed. This will require an addition to the building.

Administrative space is also a problem for First Christian. The original building was not designed for multiple staff. The result is that most offices are scattered throughout the building in rooms not designed for staff work. The church needs an administrative suite immediately to provide adequate office space for a growing staff.

Multiple use of space will provide a short-term solution to this problem. Adjacent to the offices of the pastor and secretary is a large room currently used for adult activities through the week. This room can be converted to an administrative complex by installing dividers that create five work stations for pastoral and support staff. To provide staff with privacy for counseling and other conferences, some of the Sunday school rooms can be refurnished to serve as conference rooms without interference with their use on Sunday.

The adult programs that have used this space can be moved to another large room now used only for children's Sunday school. By refurnishing that area with adjustable-height folding tables and with chairs for both children and adults, the children can use the room on Sundays and the adults during the week. The key to making this work is to use an adjacent room to store projects, equipment, and the furniture not in use at the time. Meeting long-term space needs for administration, education, and music will require a major addition several years in the future. But the short-term needs can be met by using existing space more creatively. As the facility planning committee's report to the congregation explained: "Our first goal is to fully utilize the present facility, while we plan to accommodate significant long-term growth. There is no need for major alteration or additions to the structure until full utilization of the present facility is realized." That committee understands the principle of use.

To prepare for growth, First Christian must also find a way to park more cars. Eventually the church may want to consider buying more property, but the immediate solution is offsite parking. Within three to five blocks of the church is more than enough public parking to meet the church's needs. By providing shuttle service from those areas, the church can expand its parking for a fraction of the cost of buying expensive downtown property. Some leaders have already volunteered to park offsite to leave the most convenient parking places for visitors.

While your church's space needs are different from First Christian's, the process of planning for space needs will be much the same. Determine space needs, short-term and long-term, for each ministry program. See which needs can be met by more creatively using your present space through such means as holding multiple worship services, multiple Sunday schools, and make multiple use of educational, fellowship, administrative, and worship space. Only when you have determined what your present building will do when fully utilized can you know what additional space you need and which changes need to come first.

3. Draw up a master plan

Your facilities master plan should address all your facility needs, from the immediate to the long-term, without sacrificing architectural unity. It may include the following needs:

to catch up on maintenance (such as replacing electrical wiring);

to modernize (such as making it accessible to the handicapped);

to do minor remodeling (such as knocking out walls to make a bigger nursery area);

to make modest additions (such as an enlarged foyer);

to make major additions (such as a three-story complex).

First Christian's master plan includes three additions to its present facility. The first will be an enlarged foyer area to care for the traffic created by double worship services. This addition will incorporate a handicap-access ramp and conveniently located restrooms that include handicap facilities.

The second addition will require a major building program. The main floor of this three-story complex will meet long-term needs for administrative space, doubling the space now available. The upper floor will provide additional space for an extensive music ministry, an area increasingly important for this church. The lower floor will be a multi-purpose area with movable walls that can be used for activities such as Sunday school, fellowship, and preschool. It will also serve as a support area for the adjacent sunken outdoor terrace. Now seldom used, this terrace will be improved so it can be used for such activities as weddings, picnics, and receptions. The church's growth will probably make this facility necessary within the next five years.

The third addition will be a two-story complex to meet long-term needs as the church grows and develops new ministries.

The architect's task is to so blend the changes and additions with the original building that most people will think the remodel was part of the original architect's master plan. If your existing building is not a good design, however, you will want to challenge your architect to improve the design of the entire complex in the remodeling process.

At First Christian Church architectural unity will be achieved by matching the brick in the original building, repeating the same decorative details in the brickwork, using the same roof levels on additions as are on the original building, and using the same kinds of supporting columns and overhangs. Even the walkways have unique patterns that will be duplicated.

At the same time, it is not practical or desirable to build today exactly the same kind of building that would have been built fifty years ago. While the building should blend in as if it were part of the original master plan, it must also be fully useful today. So, as the consultant at First Christian I had to ask myself, "If Saarinen were designing this building *today,* how would he do it?"

My answer was that he would use materials that are in common use today and would meet today's code and safety requirements. He would design educational space based on educational concepts now used for a growing, larger church like First Christian. Rather than use asphalt tile, which he used fifty years ago, he would use carpet. A professional like Saarinen would know carpet costs less to maintain and is more beautiful, comfortable, warm, quiet, and available. We know this is the approach Saarinen would take, because it's what he did in his day. He just did it better than most architects.

While preserving architectural unity is important and achievable, it is not possible for the building to remain the same in every detail if it is to be the kind of living structure needed to serve a growing congregation and a changing community.

4. Develop implementation plans

If extensive changes are needed, you won't be able to make them all at once. The next step, then, is to set priorities.

Where do you begin? The first changes will fall into two categories: (1) changes you can make quickly and economically, and (2) those that address your most pressing needs.

At First Christian, for example, the new administrative area can be created simply by new dividers to create work stations, a few refurnished Sunday school rooms to double as conference rooms, and new chairs and adjustable tables for the educational area. Compared to the cost of building an office complex, these expenses are minor. These changes, both urgent and relatively inexpensive, will be made first.

Another pressing need at First Christian is to make the building safe by bringing it up to present fire and electrical wiring codes. This will be an early priority.

Some changes, however, cost so much that even if they are needed now they may have to wait. First Christian faces that reality because of having to replace the heating, ventilation, and air conditioning system, which may cost as much as $750,000. The facilities committee recommends that the church continue to patch the present system for a few more years until the congregation is able to pay for a new one.

First Christian's three additions to its present facility will be phased in as they are needed and funds become available. The master plan gives priority to those changes that can be made quickly and inexpensively and those that must be made immediately to meet pressing needs. Other changes may have to be postponed based on the church's ability to pay, and yet others will be scheduled for future years to meet long-term needs.

5. Adopt a financial plan

The facilities committee at First Christian, in their report to the congregation, explained that any facilities plan submitted would "be consistent with the *ability* of the congregation to fully fund such a plan." How is the congregation's ability to fund a building project to be measured? There are two key indicators. First, can the congregation afford to remodel or add on without taking funds away from "people ministries"? If the church cuts back on ministry to people to build bigger or better facilities, it has forgotten its mission. Its priorities have been turned upside down.

Second, is the congregation prepared to pay for the project with little or no debt? The major advantage of remodeling in stages is that the church is better able to pay for the improvements as they are made and so save the interest. (Chapters 8 through 10 describe in more detail how to develop a financial plan for building or remodeling consistent with these principles.)

First Christian Church's experience is an example of a good plan for remodeling, with one exception: No church should wait fifty years to remodel. Rather, remodeling should be a continual process that results in a "living building" that changes to meet the changing needs of the congregation and community, so that the building is always the most effective ministry tool possible.

7

Is Your Church Open for Business?

Jerry awoke Monday morning with suicide on his mind. He'd been thinking about it for two months. Today he was going to *do* something about it.

He dressed quickly and, leaving the house unlocked, jumped into his car. He'd already picked out the spot—the ten-foot concrete wall at the end of Eighth Street. People will think it's an accident, he told himself. Brake failure, they'll say.

Six minutes later he turned onto Eighth Street. Four blocks ahead loomed the wall. Tires squealed and engine roared as he flattened the pedal to the floor. Twenty-five miles an hour . . . 30 . . . 40 . . . 45 . . . two blocks to go.

Just then something caught the corner of Jerry's eye. His foot came up, eased over on the brake. Only slowly did it dawn on Jerry that what he had seen, what had prompted him to lift his foot from the pedal, was a glimpse of the neighborhood church on Ninth Street that his wife and girls had attended before they left him.

A minute later he turned off the engine in front of the church building. Aloud Jerry said, "I don't know if this'll do any good, but I guess it's worth a try. If it doesn't help, well, that wall's not going anywhere."

Jerry tried the front door of the building. It was locked. He walked around to the side. Locked there, too. Another door at the back of the building didn't look worth trying. Because of the car in the parking lot and the light on inside, Jerry tried once more; he rattled several windows. No response. "Well, whaddaya know!" He pounded a window with his fist. "Not open for business."

As he walked back toward the front of the building, he noticed the church sign. "I suppose I could at least call the pastor." But when he got to the sign there was no phone number, and where the pastor's name belonged he found only the shadow left by the now-removed plastic letters of some former pastor's name. With an oath Jerry kicked the sign.

Back in his car he turned the key, shifted into reverse, and backed into the road. As he pulled away from the church, his car was headed for Eighth Street.

While this story is fictional, the situation it illustrates is not. It is not uncommon for someone seeking the church's ministry at a time other than the church's regular worship services to find it "not open for business." Just as a well-designed, wisely used building can be a valuable ministry tool, a poorly designed or improperly used building can erect barriers to ministry.

Take, for example, a church in upstate New York that asked me to help them develop a facilities plan. To reach the church secretary's office I had to enter the front door, pass through the auditorium, climb stairs, go through a balcony, and finally open the door into the bell tower. The other offices were equally well hidden. The pastor's office was in the far corner of the sanctuary off the platform. The youth pastor's office was in a windowless room off a dimly lit basement hallway. None of the offices were identified.

The front door was kept locked even during office hours. If someone pushed the door buzzer and the secretary was in—which was less than half the time and not on any particular schedule—she would come down from the bell tower and open the door. Otherwise a person seeking help might never get in, even if the pastors were there.

Not being open for business does not necessarily mean, then, that no one is staffing the church office. It may mean that the door is locked during office hours. Or that the church office entrance is not clearly marked. Or that no emergency telephone number is posted.

To fully use a church building is to use all the space for ministry seven days a week. This also means using the building effectively, as a tool for making the ministries of the church easily accessible to the community. When a church uses its building wisely seven days a week and its ministries are easily accessible to the community, then it is open for business.

To find out how open for business your church is, answer the following twenty-one questions.

An "Open for Business" Inventory

_____ 1. Do you have an outdoor sign that directs people to the church offices?

_____ 2. Is the door leading to the office area always unlocked during office hours?

_____ 3. Once a person enters the building, is it obvious how to find the offices?

_____ 4. Is the hallway leading to the office area well lighted?

_____ 5. Are all the offices for professional and support staff in the same area for maximum accessibility to the public?

_____ 6. Is your church office open regular hours?

_____ 7. Are your office hours posted?

_____ 8. Is the pastor normally available at specific hours during the week?

_____ 9. Do you have a comfortable waiting area for visitors to your church office?

_____ 10. Does the person who answers your phone and receives your visitors, whether paid or volunteer, make each caller and visitor feel like an important person rather than like an interruption?

_____ 11. Has the person who answers your phone and receives visitors, whether paid or volunteer, been trained to make referrals for physical, emotional, and spiritual crises?

_____ 12. a. Does your church have a yellow pages listing?

_____   b. If so, does it include a map that shows where the church building is?

_____   c. Does it list your office hours?

_____ 13. Are the pastors' names on the church sign?

_____ 14. Is a twenty-four-hour emergency telephone number listed

_____ 15. Does the church phone have an answering service or answering machine that gives after-hours callers a number for emergencies?

_____ 16. Do those who cannot attend Sunday services because of work have an opportunity to attend a worship service at an alternate time?

_____ 17. Do you offer more than one kind of worship to minister to different segments of your community?

_____ 18. Do you have small groups intentionally structured to incorporate new people?

_____ 19. Do you run a weekly ad in the church section of your local newspaper?

_____ 20. Do you place small but significant advertising in other sections of your local newspaper that tell about specialized ministries of your church (for example, a divorce support group)? Or do you advertise on TV or on radio stations other than Christian stations?

_____ 21. Are the foyers of your building designed so people outside can see people inside and so see when you are "open for business"?

Now count your *yes* responses. Include *yes* responses to 12b and 12c as bonus points. If your church's score is:

17–21 your "open" sign is shining bright!

11–16 you usually are open but have room to improve.

6–10 anyone determined enough can probably find you—eventually.

0– 5 your church may be your town's best-kept secret.

The inventory measures how open for business your church is in these three situations:

Questions 1 through 11 reflect how available you are to *a person* not well acquainted with your church *who comes to the office seeking help.*

Questions 10 through 15 indicate how well prepared you are to respond to *someone trying to reach you by telephone,* particularly in a crisis.

Questions 16 through 21 suggest how much effort your church makes, beyond the usual worship services, to reach out to *people who might attend public meetings.*

Notice where most of your *yes* and *no* answers fall. To which of these three groups are you most available? Which are you least prepared to serve? Which *no* responses point to ways your church could become more open for business?

It was because they wanted to correct problems like these that the upstate New York church asked me to suggest alternatives. After studying their needs I suggested several changes, not only in use of facilities but also in design. This particular church converted the parsonage next door to the church building into an administrative center with offices for the secretary and pastors. They installed a handicap ramp, put up a church office sign, posted office hours, and hired a full-time secretary/receptionist.

A few months later the secretary told me, "I'm amazed at how many people both from within and outside the congregation come through this door, people who never came by before. They come to get counseling, to request information, to share needs. I'm thrilled to get to serve all these people."

What made the difference? They were open for business.

As this church's experience illustrates, being open for business changes not only how a church uses its facilities but in most cases how it designs its facilities. A building designed to be open for business makes public access, especially access to the church offices, a top priority.

Imagine, if you will, that on a business trip, eager to reach your motel, you drive straight through till 9:00 P.M. You check into your room, then walk to the restaurant next door for your overdue dinner. The parking lot holds a single car, and the dining room is dark. As you reach the door the manager is leaving. "Can I help you?" he asks.

"I'm hungry," you say. "I've come to eat."

"Oh, I'm sorry," he says. "We're open only on Sundays and Wednesday evenings. Come back then and I'll be glad to feed you."

The church, of course, must feed people not just during two or three publicized time slots each week but any time they are hungry. When your church is accessible to hungry people seven days a week, twenty-four hours a day, then you are open for business.

The Need Test

Do You Need to Build?

Which of the following statements is true for your church? Before each statement write *yes, no,* or *NA* (for "not applicable") to your church.

Part I. Awareness of Needs

_____ 1. We know the needs of people in our community.

_____ 2. We know which of those needs we are meeting.

_____ 3. We know which additional needs we wish to minister to.

_____ 4. We have determined our short- and long-term facility needs based on present and projected ministries.

Part II. Utilization

_____ 5. Big groups are in big rooms.

_____ 6. Little groups are in little rooms.

_____ 7. The teaching methods we use maximize space use.

_____ 8. No empty spaces are left unused.

_____ 9. Seasonal storage has been moved to spaces that are not useful for people to meet or work in.

_____ 10. Furniture is arranged to get maximum use of space.

_____ 11. Furniture has been changed as needed to maximize space use.

_____ 12. Every space that can be made multi-use has been made multi-use.

_____ 13. A plan for minor remodeling to increase utilization has been or is being implemented.

_____ 14. We have multiple worship services.

_____ 15. We have multiple education sessions.

_____ 16. We have worship services on more than one day a week.

_____ 17. We have education sessions on more than one day a week.

_____ 18. If it is available, we use alternate meeting space (restaurants, offices, homes, community meeting rooms, etc.).

_____ 19. If on-site parking is inadequate, we use adjacent, remote, or stacked parking.

_____ 20. If practical in our situation, we have built or planned modest additions to increase the usefulness of our facility (for example, a fellowship foyer or administrative suite).

Interpreting Your Answers

Part I

If any of your answers to Part I are *no,* you have more research to do to determine your facility needs. Review chapter 5 for research suggestions. In changing a *no* on question 4 to a *yes,* you may find the appendix, "How to Write a Program of Needs," helpful.

If the above answers are all *yes,* you have really done your homework!

Part II

Statements 5 through 10 describe changes that can be made quickly and inexpensively. The steps described in 11 through 13 involve moderate expense. Fourteen through 17 relate to scheduling. Eighteen through 20 describe steps that can be taken, short of a new building, as you approach the use limits of your facility. Building an addition (item 20) involves substantial expense, though still far less than a new building.

How does this test tell you when you need to build?

First, before you can know if you need to build, you have to know your needs. That means you have to be able to answer yes to items 1 through 4.

Second, you need to have implemented all the applicable steps described in items 5 through 13. That means you should have only *yes* and *NA* answers for this section.

Third, you should be able to answer *yes* to at least two of the four scheduling items, numbers 14 to 17.

Finally, you should be able to answer *yes* to any of the last three items (18 through 20) that apply to your situation.

That means if you have more than two *no* answers, or if you have any *no* answers on any items other than 14 through 17, you probably don't need to build yet. Each *no* indicates a possible opportunity to more fully use existing space to provide room for growth. These *no* answers can guide your planning as you seek alternatives to building. Only when you have exercised all these options, changing your *no* answers to *yes* answers, will you need to build. Remember the principle of use: A church does not need more space until it is fully using the space it already has.

A church that has only a few *no* answers and is taking steps that will soon change them to *yes* answers is probably approaching full use of its facilities. If that is your situation, you need to be preparing a master site plan that will tell you how much growth you can accommodate at your present site through full utilization of facilities and additional construction. Relocation is usually the most expensive and least desirable option, a last resort appropriate only when the present site, intensively utilized, does not allow for significant growth. Even in that case, creative alternatives, such as starting satellite congregations, can be considered.

What if your church has passed the motivation test, and has passed, or soon will, the need test? Is it time to build? Not necessarily. There is yet one more test—the finances test. No matter how pure its motives, no matter how much it needs to build, a church must not build before it is financially ready. If it does— and many churches do—it usually cripples its ministries, often slows or stops its growth, and may even put the future of the church at risk. The next three chapters illustrate these dangers and show how your church can avoid them by following biblical financial principles.

The Principle of Provision

A church should build
only when it can do so
within the income God has provided
and without using funds
needed for the church's present
and future ministries to people.

8

Good Intentions Are Not Enough

One of the most exciting jobs I've ever had as an architect was designing the campus for a growing church on the West Coast. A group of men in this church, all successful businessmen with extensive experience in development, all of them spiritual leaders, had put together an unusually creative plan for building on a new site. Rather than just buying land for the church and building the buildings, these businessmen, in partnership with the church, bought land for a large new residential development. The church campus was a carefully planned part of the development, designed to enable the church to provide a variety of services to the community. The concept was strictly state of the art.

Added to this was an innovative method for financing the building. All the profits from the development would go to help pay the costs for land and construction of the church. The existing church building would be sold to pay the balance, and the people would move into their new building debt free, with plenty of money for ministry and growth.

Working with the building committee was a delight. I found among the committee members a strong faith and beautiful spirit. Their vision was not only to build a building but to build the church as well. I would leave our work sessions with my faith encouraged, thankful for the privilege of working with such an inspiring team. You can understand my excitement, then, when the model homes were built, bringing closer the sale of the future homes and the building of the new church campus.

But then an unexpected flaw appeared in what had seemed an otherwise perfect plan: The local economy collapsed. The area had been expanding, new homes had been selling well. But as the local job supply plummeted, people began to move out of the area. The developers did everything possible to rescue the project, but it was still forced into bankruptcy. All the time the church leaders had put into planning was wasted. All the money the congregation had invested was lost. This creative, exciting plan ended in disaster.

"Lord, how could you let this happen?" I asked. "These people are so sincere and so dedicated to you. Their motives and goals were so right. Why this?"

I walked away from that job with sadness, frustration, and unanswered questions. My grief deepened over the years as I watched the church lose momentum and members, for it spent almost ten years paying the debt on a building it never built.

Eventually I realized what had gone wrong. The church had chosen an unscriptural plan to pay for its building. Rather than rely on the giving of the people, the church had invested in a business enterprise, a business enterprise that was not the work of the church. The motivation was right, but the method was wrong. Good intentions had not been enough.

They never are. Whenever the church operates in the world's economic system, it experiences the consequences of that choice. In this case, the church happened to get onto the world's economic roller coaster just before it started a rapid decline.

But suppose the church's timing had been better and the economic roller coaster had continued to climb for a while as the developers had expected it would. What if the church had been able to build debt free and without having to ask the congregation for donations to pay for the building?

That outcome would have created its own problems. The whole plan was based on the prospect of the church's getting something without the people having to pay for it. It was, in effect, a type of get-rich-quick scheme, something Scripture strongly cautions against: "The man who wants to get rich quick will quickly fail" (Prov. 28:20). Such an approach to the church's work takes ownership away from the people. It undermines their commitment to support the church.

Investing in business enterprises is only one way the church can substitute a worldly method of funding for a biblical plan of provision. Another far more common way churches fall into this trap is through borrowing.

Scripture does not call borrowing sin, but it does call it slavery: "The rich rules over the poor, and the borrower is the slave of the lender" (Prov. 22:7 NRSV). When a church borrows, the mortgage payment then takes priority over all other financial commitments. The church becomes a slave to the lender, placing itself under an authority other than God's.

Whenever I analyze a church's finances and discover that their financial priorities are out of balance, almost always the culprit is debt. Debt allows us to live beyond our means, to build on our schedule rather than God's. Getting ahead of God can hinder the church's outreach or even so cripple the church's ministry that people are driven away.

A congregation of 250 decided to build a sanctuary to seat six hundred. The written financial plan the church presented to the lender was based on three stated assumptions. First, it assumed that because of the building program the church would grow and bring in new givers. Second, it assumed that, motivated by the building program, present and future members would increase their per capita giving. Third, it assumed that the prevailing boom economy would continue, and that rapid inflation would enable the congregation to pay back their loan with much cheaper dollars. Based on these highly questionable assumptions, the lender awarded the loan.

Once the building was complete, however, the growth never came. The boom economy went bust. Instead of new people coming to the church, people left, because they did not want to be on a sinking ship. Even with increased giving, those who remained could not make the mortgage payments, and the lending institution foreclosed.

This church's most obvious mistake was to borrow more than the existing congregation could repay. This practice almost always creates debt so heavy that the church's focus changes from ministry to mortgage payments, and that in itself stops church growth, as happened with this church.

But speculative business ventures and borrowing against future growth are not the only ways to endanger a church's future; even conservative borrowing can put a church's ministries at unnecessary risk.

A church in Oregon built a new building, taking care to borrow no more than the existing congregation could repay. Soon after the building was completed, the major industry in town, a lumber mill, shut down. Many church members had to relocate to other communities to find work. Many who remained became dependent upon unemployment benefits or were underemployed. For years to come, the church's primary focus became the repayment of debt.

Since we all live in a credit-driven economy, we may have trouble even imagining any way to finance building other than debt. But the world's way is not God's way. God tells us to be content with what we have (Heb. 13:5; 1 Tim. 6:6-8). Borrowing is a way to get things sooner than we could without borrowing. It expresses discontentment with what God has provided.

God has promised to provide all our needs (Phil. 4:19). When the church borrows to build, it says, perhaps unintentionally, that God cannot be trusted to supply the church's need at the time of the need. Larry Burkett, founder and president of Christian Financial Concepts, puts it this way: "The very act of borrowing is the outer sign of an inner doubt. . . . It does not necessarily represent an overt sin, but it does reflect that a church is willing to accept the *least* financially rather than the *best*. . . . Assuming it is God's will for a church to build, He will supply the resources to do it."[1]

Virgil Vogt recommends prayer as an alternative to borrowing: "If our need or project is legitimate, why can't we simply ask God for the necessary resources and expect to receive them?. . . He is eager and ready to respond. And if we ask, but do not receive, perhaps the project is ill-conceived. Can we take no for an answer and still be content? If we borrow, we withhold from God opportunities to bless us and supply our needs. And sometimes we may deny him the opportunity to say no to a project."[2]

FIGURE 2

Disadvantages of Church Debt	Advantages of Church Debt
1. It's difficult to motivate people to pay debt.	1. It gives the church freedom to move ahead with its own plans in its own time without waiting on God to provide.
2. The church assumes all the risks of indebtedness without benefiting from any of the advantages of business debt: appreciation, depreciation, tax advantages, leverage, etc.	
3. It gambles the very future of the church on uncertain future events.	
4. The church becomes slave to the lender.	
5. Money that should have been spent on ministry is diverted to pay interest.	
6. Borrowing allows the church to live beyond its means.	
7. Debt tends to destroy our peace.	

When the church borrows, then, it puts itself under the lender's authority, exhibits a lack of contentment with what God has provided, and substitutes debt for trust in God. But that's not all. It also wastes money, often large amounts of money, that could better be used for the real work of the church. Depending on how much is borrowed, at what interest rate, and for how long, borrowing to build can double or triple the cost of building.

Take, for example, a church that builds a $200,000 building and borrows the money at 12 percent interest on a fifteen-year note. The total cost of the building over fifteen years will be $432,000, of which $232,000 is interest.

Suppose, though, that this church decides not to borrow. Instead they find ways to use their existing building more fully so they can continue to grow while they save for their new building. Each month they set aside $2,400 (the amount their monthly mortgage payment would have been) for their building fund, where it earns 10 percent interest. After five years and four months, the church has set aside $152,000 and has earned another $48,000 interest for a total of $200,000. They are ready to build for cash.

If the church borrows to build, it will take fifteen years and $432,000 of giving to pay for the building. If they save to pay cash, it will take them only five years and four months, and $152,000 of giving. By paying cash the church cuts building costs by 65 percent and frees up $2,400 a month for almost ten years—a total of $280,000—for the church's ministries.

For simplicity's sake, this example uses constant dollars. In an inflationary economy the savings realized by saving to build for cash would be somewhat less. For example, if the cost of building increased $60,000 during the savings period, building for cash would free up only $220,000 rather than $280,000. To prevent the savings period from being lengthened by the effects of inflation, I recommend that churches set aside not a flat dollar amount but a fixed percentage of church income for any upcoming major building program. This ties the building fund to both inflation and the growth of the church. If the church grows faster

FIGURE 3

Building With Debt

Construction Cost: $200,000
Interest Rate (15-year note): 12%*
Monthly Mortgage Payments: $1,200

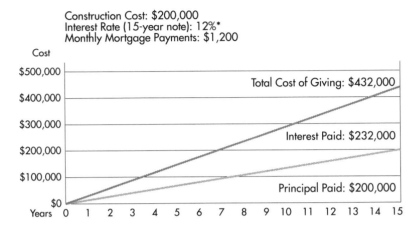

Building With Provision

Construction Cost: $200,000
Interest Earned on Savings: 10%*
Monthly Investment in Provision Fund: $1,200

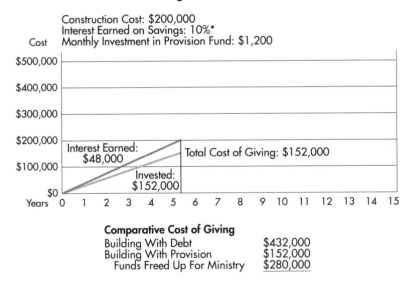

Comparative Cost of Giving

Building With Debt	$432,000
Building With Provision	$152,000
Funds Freed Up For Ministry	$280,000

* Interest rates are for illustrative purposes only. Use current interest rates to calculate your actual costs.

than projected and so needs to build sooner than planned, it will also have enough funds saved sooner than planned.

While the church must operate within the world's economic system, it does not have to operate by the world's principles. When a church follows a financial plan based solidly on biblical principles, it is largely insulated from the ups and downs of the economy, and so its work, present and future, is safeguarded.

These principles are no secret. They have been tried. They work. The next chapter shows how one church applied them.

9

From Debt to Provision

Years ago when I began to work with a church, I asked two questions: How long has it been since you built? and, How much is your debt? If they had not built within the last ten years and if they were not in debt, I would scold them.

"What you need to do," I would say, "is have a building program every ten years. Take out a ten-year mortgage. Once it's paid off, start the process all over again." I became an expert not only at helping churches get loans but at telling them the maximum debt they could carry and still stay afloat. While my advice was obviously in the best interest of the architect (me), not to mention the lender, I also sincerely believed it was in the best interest of the church.

I now know that my advice reflected not biblical teaching but the world's values. While borrowing money violates no explicit "Thou shalt not," the Bible does consistently view debt negatively and never as part of God's plan for the church.

Many church leaders assume that borrowing to build is inevitable. But churches that have chosen to base their finances on the principle of provision—the confidence that God has promised to provide all the church's needs as the needs arise— have discovered that facility needs can be met without debt and that building debt-free greatly reduces the cost of building. This makes more money available for ministry, which in turn often translates into more effective outreach. In fact, a church that follows the principle of provision can be in the middle of a major building program—building for cash—and at the same time launch new outreach ministries. A Philadelphia congregation, Fairview Church of the Nazarene, shows how.

When the church was organized in 1969 with seventy-five people, they made several good financial decisions. They bought an adequate seventeen-acre site at a reasonable cost in a good location—a rural community destined to become heavily residential. They built a building they could afford for administration, nursery, classrooms, and worship space seating about 250. As the church grew, they added a second unit, a totally multipurpose residential-style building with a meeting hall and kitchen upstairs and classrooms in the walkout half-basement. The fellowship hall was divided into classrooms by folding walls and was used by the church-operated preschool and elementary school.

By the time they asked me to work with them in 1981 they were desperate for space. The first time I entered the building, I opened the front door to find the floor of the foyer covered with school children on pallets. I made my way to the hall, which was filled with school equipment and furniture and more sleeping children whom I had to step over to reach the office. Without question this church was open for business, but this was a case of the tail wagging the dog; the school was overrunning the church. In fact, during school hours the church had no space for its other ministry activities.

On Sunday morning I found the auditorium packed, even with the children worshiping separately from the adults. Parking overflowed onto the field behind the church. Every classroom was full. Clearly, this church's space needs had to be addressed at once.

You already know part of what happened next. This church, whose story was introduced in chapter 1, wanted me to design a thousand-seat sanctuary. Before I visited the church, that's what I intended to do. But after studying their finances I became convinced that a major building program would cripple the church's ministries and stop its rapid growth. Still in debt from their previous building, the congregation simply did not have the funds to take on a major building program without taking money away from present and future ministry to people. Building would have changed the focus of the church.

Fortunately, the church did not need to build. By applying the principle of use—fully utilizing present facilities before adding more space—the church could postpone building for several years. Step by step, then, here is how Fairview Village applied the principle of *use,* moved from financing by debt to financing by *provision,* and in the process managed to keep the church's *focus* on ministry to people.

1. The church met immediate space needs through better utilization of facilities. They went to double worship services. They built a storage shed that let them empty out three Sunday school rooms. Bigger classes were moved to bigger rooms and smaller classes to smaller rooms. Chairs replaced pews, converting the worship area into multi-use space. A barn that received only limited use was remodeled to make it usable for their elementary school, Sunday school, and week-night activities. These changes, along with a cap on school enrollment, enabled the school to move back into appropriate boundaries and freed up rooms for the church to use on weekdays.

2. The leaders presented a total financial plan to the congregation. The plan's goal was to get the church out of debt and onto a provision plan that met all the facility and ministry needs of the church.

3. The people increased their giving to get out of debt. Through increased giving, the congregation became debt free in less than a year without endangering funding for staff and ministry.

4. The congregation began to save for the next phase of their facility plan. While they continued to set aside the same percentage of giving income they had been using to retire their debt, the church began to draw up plans for remodeling and a modest addition.

Since the remodeling was already overdue, the church's goal was to pay cash for half of this building project and make the transition to a provision economy with the next phase. The church called this "almost provision." Seldom is it possible for a church to move from a debt economy to a provision economy in a single step.

5. The church completed the needed remodeling and a modest addition. Removing the wall between the worship area and foyer increased worship seating from 250 to 300. A large fellowship foyer and an administrative suite were added. The foyer not only facilitated traffic flow and fellowship between worship services but doubled as a meeting room. Church offices just off the foyer made the church more open for business by making the staff more accessible to the public during the week. These changes gave the church room to grow to 600 with double services.

6. The church continued to set aside the same percentage of income for the building fund. Because the church was setting aside a percentage of giving for the building fund rather than a flat dollar amount, the monthly income to the building fund increased as the church grew and giving increased. Within two years after the completion of the remodeling, the church was once again debt free.

The monthly amount that had been going to pay debt then went into the building fund in preparation for the next phase of the facility plan—a major two-story building scheduled to be built in five years. The lower level would be used for both the elementary school and children's Sunday school. The upper level would be a large multipurpose room with a soundproof movable wall system that made it possible to divide the space into rooms of various sizes and configurations for education and fellowship.

7. The church completed its transition to a "provision" economy. The church grew faster than anticipated, with an average attendance of 850 by 1989, so a third service was added and the next building was built sooner than planned. Of the $1.2 million construction cost, $850,000 was on hand when construction began, and the rest was raised during construction, which enabled the church to complete this major building program debt free. This was accomplished just eight years after the church had committed itself to live within its income.

With the principle of provision fully implemented, the church can now continue to set aside the same percentage for building. By the time they need the thousand-seat worship area they originally asked me to design, they can be ready to build it, too, without borrowing.

This church's continued rapid growth shows that it is possible to continue to reach out effectively even while building. In fact, about the same time their $1.2 million building program was getting underway, the church was offered the use of a building in an adjacent low-income neighborhood. Because the church had so planned their building program that it would take no funds away from ministry, they were financially ready to say yes to this opportunity to launch an exciting new multifaceted ministry, even as the building was going up.

This was possible for two reasons. First, by applying the *principle of use,* over the years the congregation had moved from using most of their space for single use to using almost all their space for multiple uses. As a result, the number of square feet needed per person had been cut by at least 40 percent, which in turn cut construction costs by that same amount.

Second, by applying the *principle of provision,* living within the income God provided to the church, they were able to eventually pay cash for a major building program and then eliminate all the interest expense which, in this case, would have

been about 60 percent of the total construction cost had the
church taken out a conventional twenty-year note.

In these two ways the church saved over 75 percent of construction costs as compared with traditional single-use construction and debt financing. As a result, the church was able to
continue to grow and to expand its outreach even during a major
building program.

Almost any growing church that consistently applies the principles of use and provision can achieve similar savings, though
the percentage of construction costs saved will vary depending
on the church's specific circumstances and the economic cli-
mate. If all the churches of North America would fully use existing space before adding more space and would move from debt
financing to provision financing, total spending on church construction could be cut by more than half, and many billions of
dollars every year would be saved.

As impressive as that would be, elimination of spending for
unnecessary buildings will not in itself make much difference
in the church's effectiveness. To capitalize on the tremendous
opportunity created when it drastically cuts spending for buildings, the church must redirect those funds to the real work of
the church—ministering to people's needs. How to do that is
the subject of the next chapter.

10

Turning Church Spending Right Side Up

The best outward indicator of a person's priorities may be how that person spends money. The same is true of churches. How a church spends its money tells what is most important to that church.

When I worked with a Baptist church in Brewster, New York, I discovered guests in many homes: displaced persons, runaways, people in crisis. No one who came to the church needing food was turned away, and a house behind the church provided a night's lodging for those who had nowhere else to stay.

As the church's outreach to homeless people grew, the ministry needed a larger building. Some people in the congregation laid hands on a nearby building that housed a bar and was used by prostitutes. They prayed and claimed the building for the Lord's work. You can guess what happened. The bar closed, the prostitutes moved, and the owner turned the building over to the church.

This congregation's priorities were clear to me, not only because of where they invested their time but also because of how they spent their money.

The New Testament shows us the financial priorities of the early church. Caring for the needy within the Christian community was the church's top financial priority (Acts 2:44–45; 4:32, 34–35; 6:1–6; 2 Cor. 8–9). Giving to the needy outside the community of faith was also essential to New Testament faith (Gal. 6:10; Matt. 25:31–46). Even two centuries after these verses were written, in A.D. 250 the relatively small church at Rome gave regular support to fifteen hundred distressed persons, probably spending more than 80 percent of the church's income on relief.

Of that period of church history it was written: "Everybody was expected to seek out, street by street, the poorest dwellings of strangers, with the result that the Christians spent more money in the streets than the followers of other religions spent in their temples. . . .What struck and astounded the outside observer the most was the extent to which poverty was overcome in the vicinity of the communities. This was achieved by their voluntary work of love, which had nothing to do with the more or less compulsory social welfare of the state."[1]

The churches also financially supported apostles (1 Cor. 9), and some pastor-teachers may have received limited support, though pastors were not salaried (Gal. 6:6; 1 Tim. 5:18). The financial priorities of the early church, then, were (1) to meet the financial needs of those within the local body, (2) to meet the financial needs of believers in other places, (3) to meet the financial needs of local non-Christians, and (4) to provide financial support for apostles (missionaries) and perhaps some pastoral leaders.

Conspicuous by its absence is mention of money spent on facilities, especially since at that time Jews and followers of other religions spent substantial sums on places of worship. To choose not to build worship facilities flew in the face of society's conventional wisdom.

How do the financial priorities of the New Testament church compare with those of most churches today? A typical North American congregation spends anywhere from 25 percent to 55 percent of its budget on facilities, including mortgage payments and the maintenance and operation of buildings. Salaries typically require another 30 percent to 50 percent or more. Then comes giving to various denominational agencies and overseas missions. Usually less than 10 percent is left for the various ministry programs of the local church. It is rare for a church to spend more than 3 percent of its budget for intentional local outreach and to meet the needs of people in its own community. Most churches have little or no money budgeted specifically for benevolence or local outreach of any kind.

While meeting the needs of hurting people within the congregation and in the surrounding community was the top financial priority for the New Testament church, such needs rarely receive more than a token amount of North American church budgets today. In most cases, building and paying for buildings has replaced meeting people's needs as the church's top spending priority.

The only way to turn the church's financial priorities right side up again is to sharply cut spending on buildings and sharply increase spending on the needs of people within the congregation and in the local community. While churches also need to give to people far away, it is important not to let check writing become a substitute for personal involvement in the lives of those being helped. One way to keep this from happening is for a congregation always to budget at least as much for local ministries in which church members are personally involved as they do for ministries to people "far away."

The New Testament sets an example not only in spending priorities but also in generosity. After analyzing the finances of many churches of different sizes, in different locations, and of many denominations I have found a clear relationship between the generosity of congregations and their vitality and growth.

A maintenance church, for example, one that is not growing, can operate on a giving level as low as 3 percent of its members' income. Because it does not grow, that is all it needs. A church with a giving level of 5 percent to 6 percent will usually have enough funding to support modest growth. For a church to enjoy continuous significant growth, its members will have to give 8 percent to 10 percent of their income. If the members of a church give 10 percent or more of their income, the church will have enough income to meet all the needs of a growing church, including building needs, provided the facilities are fully utilized as described in chapter 5.

As important as generous giving is, and as important as it is to sharply cut building expenses, those two factors alone will not produce effective outreach. The people of the congregation must also have a compassion for hurting people and a vision for how to respond to their needs.

I recommended to a church in Montana that they increase their spending on intentional outreach. One gentleman raised his hand and asked, "If we had more money to spend for intentional outreach, what would we spend it on?" He honestly had no idea. Yet, in that town were thousands of university students, and the church spent not a nickel to reach out to that campus. Next door to the church was a large apartment complex filled with middle-income families, yet no one from that complex attended the church. That congregation's opportunities for intentional outreach were as great as for any church I have ever visited, yet they had no vision for how they could begin to reach out.

That is not unusual. Many churches, especially those that have become accustomed to no growth, have become blind to the needs of the people around them. If they suddenly had 10 or 15 percent of their budgets earmarked for intentional outreach, they would not know what to do with the money. How can a church effectively invest funds in local outreach?

Sunnyside Temple in Waterloo, Iowa, decided to provide a Christian teen nightclub to reach out to the youth of the community. The night I visited the club it was jammed with teens playing video and other kinds of games. A disc jockey was busy, and the soda fountain was swamped. There were more teens in the corridor and outside just enjoying being together. The Christian teens had been trained to make friends and bring them into the fellowship where they could find a place to belong and learn what it meant to follow Jesus. Sunnyside Temple's outreach to teens cost money.

A man in Sturgis, South Dakota, had a burden for teens who were in trouble with the law. Through a ministry he started in the parsonage basement he introduced them to Christ's forgiveness. The ministry grew and eventually took over the whole parsonage. The pastor had to move to a new home. This ministry to youth cost money.

The basement of the Presbyterian Church in Sligo, Pennsylvania, was filled wall to wall with clothes for all who needed them. This little western Pennsylvania coal mining town was served, the needs of many met. Because it was involved in this and other ministries of outreach, the church was growing. Outreach costs.

A business building next to the Sierra Madre Congregational Church in the Los Angeles area housed an exciting ministry. Trained lay people from the congregation, supervised by a professional, offered Christian counseling to those who came seeking help. There was a waiting line on evenings the "clinic" was open. This ministry of counseling cost money.

A church in Hayward, California, bought used video games and filled an unused room at the back of the church with them. When the room opened after school, the driveway was filled with kids of all colors, sizes, and ages. There was no charge except for refreshments.

As laughter and play filled the room, suddenly all the machines went off at once. Most of the crowd went into the fellowship hall, sat on the floor, and listened to a message told in their own language about a new life. Many spiritual needs were met. Parents came to find out what was going on, curious about reports of free fun and fellowship and the changed behavior they saw in their children. This outreach to children and their parents cost money.

"The lay ministers who are going to facilitate the new recovery support groups need training, apprenticeship, and teaching materials, such as the twelve-step curriculum," my pastor said. "We'll have to put that in our budget along with the cost of other outreach tools." In recent years our small but growing congregation of 120 has invested in a variety of outreach tools. These include the Chuck Bradley videos produced by Church Growth, Inc., that have challenged our people to reach out; Larry Burkett's workbooks and visual aids for teaching biblical finance; Elmer Towns's materials on reaching the baby boomers; and curriculum to help people identify their spiritual gifts and ministries.

Such equipping for outreach is possible because the church budgets for these needs and provides funds for a community-oriented teen outreach and a growing women's ministry. Outreach costs.

If a congregation truly wants to reach out in compassion to the people around them, and will ask God to show them outreach opportunities, God will open their eyes to a host of needs, far more than they can possibly respond to.

This raises the next question: When there are so many needs, and the church cannot respond to them all, how is a congregation to decide where to begin?

A Mennonite church in Newton, Kansas, illustrates one possible approach. Looking for ways to make outreach a higher priority, the members reviewed various needs in the community and considered ways to respond. But as they discussed options, they realized that no one in the congregation had a clear call to lead any of the proposed ministries.

The church decided to go ahead and budget an amount for an undesignated new outreach with its specific use to be determined during the year when the right opportunity arose. Sure enough, several months later a physician in the church felt led to organize a low-cost clinic for the medically underserved. Several other members of the congregation, both health professionals and lay people, joined the effort. The church then used the funds earlier set aside to help launch the clinic.

An opportunity for the church to further increase its spending for outreach came in November when the treasurer reported that giving from January through November was adequate to cover budgeted expenses for all twelve months of the year. The church then designated all December income for outreach, with the specific uses of those funds to be decided at a church meeting early the following year. This financial surplus was achieved even though the congregation consisted of only about 75 people. How was this possible? According to the pastor, it was because the church was not burdened with the expense of owning a building, but paid only a modest rent.

What does it take to turn church finances right side up? It takes a commitment to sharply reduce spending on buildings through consistently applying the principles of use and provision. It takes generous giving. It takes an awareness of needs in the community and a desire to respond to those needs compassionately. It takes a commitment to designate for benevolence and outreach those funds made available through reduced building expense and increased giving. And it takes the willingness of the people of the church to become personally involved as God directs them to give not only their money but also their time and energy to ministries that reach out to hurting people around them.

Turning church finances right side up is possible, but it is not something that can be accomplished casually. It calls for nothing less than turning the very priorities of the church right side up again.

The Finances Test

Are You Financially Ready to Build?

Which of the following are true for your church? Check those that apply.

_____ 1. The regular giving in our church is strong.

_____ 2. The giving units—individuals or families who give regularly—represent a majority of the congregation.

_____ 3. We consistently meet our budget, fully funding our ministries and staff needs.

_____ 4. Our budget includes adequate funds for intentional outreach and to meet needs of people in our community.

_____ 5. We teach biblical finance for families and individuals, including an emphasis on biblical giving.

_____ 6. The church is out of debt.

_____ 7. In a survey, the present giving units have committed themselves to an increase in their giving to cover the cost of construction and future building operation costs, so that none of the church's present ministry spending will be diverted to building.

_____ 8. The increased giving for future facilities needs has been invested in an interest-bearing provision fund.

_____ 9. The church has invested enough in its provision fund to be able to pay cash or almost cash for the proposed building program.

Interpreting Your Results

If you checked statements 1 through 6, your church is probably basically financially healthy, and by implementing steps 7, 8, and 9, you should be financially ready to build within a few years. When all nine statements are true for your church, you pass the financial readiness test.

You have now studied three principles: the principle of focus, the principle of use, and the principle of provision. You have taken three corresponding tests: the motivation test, the need test, and the finances test. Few, if any, churches will "pass" all three tests the first time they take them. That does not mean such churches do not "measure up." In most cases it means the church does not need to build yet or it needs to do more planning, growing, or saving before it launches a building program.

The results of these three tests, taken together, identify issues the church needs to address and steps the church needs to take in its facility decisions. A growing church that carefully follows these steps will eventually achieve full utilization of its existing facility and become financially prepared to build. When such a church can retake all three tests and "pass" all three, *then* it is time to build. In fact, to delay building beyond that point may hinder the church's growth.

As a church approaches the time to build, it will need to form a church-growth committee to carefully plan what kind of facility can best serve the church in its continued growth and outreach. Chapter 11 tells how to find the right people for that growth committee (they are not who you would think), and chapters 12 and 13 explain how to design a building specifically suited to the needs of the growing congregation.

Even if your church is years away from a major building program, you will find practical ideas in these next three chapters and the appendix that may help you turn your present facility into a more effective ministry tool.

When It's Time to Build

By creatively using existing facilities,
a church can grow
to two or three times the size it otherwise could,
without a major building program.
But if the church continues to grow,
the time to build will come.
When that time comes,
how does the church go about it?

11

Who Should and Who Should Not Plan Your Building

When Parkside Church outgrew their building, Pastor Smith considered himself fortunate. Though he had no training or experience in building, the congregation included several professionals in the building trades. So once the congregation voted to move ahead with a new building program, the board had no trouble appointing a building committee consisting primarily of construction professionals.

- Paul was a plumber.
- Carl was a rough-in carpenter.
- Bill built warehouses.
- Charlie was an excavator.
- Cal was a concrete contractor.
- Helen had designed her own house.
- Don was a draftsman.
- Joy was known for the interior decoration of her home.

The committee was appointed and went to work. Their first task was to design the new building. What rooms were needed? How large should they be? Where should they go? At what stage of the church's growth would each room be needed?

The options became even more complex when they started considering how to use their existing building. Not that there was any shortage of creative ideas; everyone had suggestions. After a dozen meetings, though, the committee was no closer to a decision. It became obvious that they needed to bring in a professional to put this puzzle together.

Fortunately, Bill had a good friend, Arch, who was an architect. Arch had recently designed a building for another denomination in town to replace their deteriorating older structure. With a little adaptation, Arch was able to make his "stock plan" fit with Parkside's existing building and give it a striking exterior appearance.

The church hired Bill to be the construction superintendent, and several other committee members became subcontractors. Pastor Smith occasionally mentioned from the pulpit how fortunate the church was to have so many people trained and gifted in building, and how much money it was saving the church.

But before long the committee hit some snags. Poor contractual and payment procedures caused unnecessary expenses. As construction costs escalated, an additional loan became necessary. When construction was finished, the committee found they had no funds left for furnishings, landscaping, or to pave the parking lot. Worse yet, because of the unexpectedly high debt burden, the church had to delay hiring the new associate pastor and could not replace the secretary who had just resigned.

The building had simply cost too much. And it soon became apparent that in spite of its high price, the building was still inadequate. Somehow the congregation's needs for fellowship space had been largely overlooked. And many of the rooms were too small to provide for the open room and team teaching approaches needed in the growing Sunday school classes. The problem, Pastor Smith realized in retrospect, was that Arch's plans had been designed for a static church, one that was not growing. As a growing congregation, Parkside needed a different kind of facility.

Why, Pastor Smith wondered, with so many reputable construction professionals on the building committee, had they ended up with an overpriced building so poorly suited to the congregation's needs?

The answer, surprisingly enough, is to be found in the way the building committee was selected. The story you have just read is not the story of a single church, but rather a composite story of scores of churches. While the specifics vary, this basic approach to putting together a building committee has been followed by at least 80 percent of the churches I have worked with as architect.

One church in Arkansas, for example, hired me to draw up building plans for them. The building committee included, among others, a cabinetmaker, a plumber, and a small contractor. The church ended up with really good cabinets, and the plumbing was excellent, but I was never quite sure the building fit the ministries of the church.

Is it a mistake, then, to rely on construction professionals within the congregation when the church builds? No, not at all. The skills these members bring can be extremely valuable during a building program. The problem arises when construction experts are expected to perform functions outside their areas of expertise.

The key to solving this common problem is found in the recognition that planning and construction are two distinct functions that call for two distinct sets of skills. Those best able to supervise construction are the construction experts. Those best able to decide what kind of space is needed to facilitate ministry, however, are not the construction experts but ministry experts—those who actively direct the ministry programs the building will serve.

One church on the East Coast has tried it both ways. In the early 1980s the church made a $200,000 addition to its building. Their building committee was set up the usual way, with a cabinetmaker from the congregation as chairman. The cabinetmaker (let's call him Gary) was a great guy and very well-intentioned, but he didn't have the planning skills that a $200,000 building program called for. He was not a "big picture" person. Fortunately, the church had hired an outside consultant who was able to guide the committee in the right direction on design decisions, often in spite of Gary.

But even that did not control all the damage. Gary took personal responsibility for a portion of the remodeling. Once he got into it, it became obvious that he was in over his head. The church finally had to hire someone else to come in and finish the job at a higher total cost than if they had hired a professional in the first place. Because Gary was serving outside his area of expertise, the church wasted time and money, and leaders had to resolve some sticky and unnecessary relationship problems.

A few years later the church built a million dollar building. This time, though, the responsibility to plan the new building was given to a growth task force made up of lay people and church staff who were active ministry leaders.

This task force was not so easy to appoint. Great care was taken to select those who could best identify what kinds of facilities the growing church's ministries would need in years to come. The task force included spiritual leaders active in ministries to children, youth, and adults, in the music ministry, in outreach, and in administration. It also included some whose jobs gave them an understanding of the community the church served.

The task force asked all those in the congregation with specialized construction skills to list their credentials. Those who responded became a pool of advisors whose expertise was called upon as needed during planning and construction.

In areas where the congregation had no experts, the church employed consultants. Because this church placed high priority on planning, not only did they hire architects and engineers for the construction phase, they also hired a church planning specialist to guide the task force and help them prepare their work in a form useful to the architects and engineers.

FIGURE 4

The Planning and Construction Functions in a Building Program

Committees responsible to plan the building

Committee responsible to implement building plans

There is no single right way to separate the planning function from construction. A church in Kansas City achieved the same result with another approach. They created a building council made up of ministry leaders to plan the building. Subcommittees for worship, music and drama, landscape and parking, and administration reported to this council. Each developed proposals in its area of specialty.

The construction experts—plumbers, building contractors, and so on—were not found on either the building council or any of its planning subcommittees. They served instead on another subcommittee called the construction committee. Once the council had defined what kind of facility was needed, it became the construction committee's responsibility to implement those plans by hiring the architects and engineers and overseeing actual construction.

By separating planning and construction functions, this church has involved both ministry experts and construction experts where they can make their greatest contributions without expecting either to make decisions outside their areas of expertise.

The key, then, to putting together an effective building team is the same principle that should guide all aspects of staffing the church's work: Match people's abilities to the corresponding responsibilities. When applied to a building program, the principle works like this:

1. To plan the kind of facilities that can best serve your present and future ministries and to write your program of facility needs (see appendix), call on your ministry experts. I like to call this group the church-growth committee.

2. To oversee construction of your building, call on your construction experts.

3. For any aspects of your building program, either planning or construction, for which you do not have experts within the congregation, hire outside professionals.

By using this approach in their most recent building, the East Coast church avoided the problems they had had last time. Neither Gary nor any of the other construction specialists experienced the frustration of getting in over their heads, yet they all had opportunity to contribute their expertise. And today the congregation enjoys the use of a versatile building uniquely suited to their full schedule of ministry activities.

12

Designing Your Facilities for Multiple Use

Traditionally, church buildings have been designed as single-use facilities. The sanctuary is used for worship, classrooms for Christian education, the fellowship hall for dinners, the gymnasium for recreation. This is how church architects, including me, have been trained to build. For many years that was how I designed buildings, and because I worked mostly with non-growing congregations, that approach served both me and the congregations well.

But once I began to work mostly with growing churches, I ran into a problem: Single-use architecture and continuing growth just don't mix. As today's fastest-growing congregations have discovered, to build single-use buildings fast enough to keep pace with their space needs is usually prohibitively expensive. Even when it is possible, growing churches discover again and again that unnecessary building programs siphon away from the real work of the church the very time, money, and

119

energy that have made its ministries effective and stimulated its growth. When that happens growth usually slows or stops.

To meet the needs of the growing church and preserve its growing edge, a different kind of architecture is needed, one for which most architects have not been trained. The growing church needs not a single-use facility but a multi-use facility—one where almost every space is designed to be used for multiple functions seven days a week.

My work with growing churches has forced me to abandon many of my traditional design ideas and to adopt—often from the churches I work with—designs with innovative multi-use features. Here are the most important of those features.

The Ministry Center

I used to believe that worship services should take place in a sanctuary, a holy place set apart exclusively for the worship of God. In my work with growing churches, though, I discovered that most of them did not have enough space for all their ministries, and if they kept growing they probably never would have enough. As a consultant, I faced a choice: Either leave the worship space lying unused 90 percent of the time and tell the churches to stop growing, or find a way for these churches to use that space the other six and a half days a week.

The solution that has evolved over the years is what I call a ministry center. This is a meeting space designed for the liturgy of the church: worship, music, baptism, communion, weddings, funerals, and teaching. If the congregation wishes, the ministry center can also accommodate drama, concerts, films, multimedia presentations, and other special programs. Depending on the needs and desires of the congregation, it can also be designed for other ministries throughout the week: fellowship dinners, teens' and children's activities, senior citizens' programs, or school use.

The key to making the ministry center work for a wide variety of uses is movable seating: comfortable church chairs on a flat floor. This makes it possible to tailor the seating to the nature of the service or event. For example, while a center aisle is needed for weddings, side aisles work better for preaching and teaching so more people can be seated in front of the speaker. For funerals the front few rows can be removed and the family seated to one side.

With movable seating more or fewer chairs can be set up, depending on attendance, to avoid the half-empty feeling that can inhibit growth. Chairs can be arranged to form small groups for discussion, sharing, or prayer. Tables may be added for conferences, teaching, or fellowship. Seating can face different directions, be angled, or set up "in the round." Continental seating—rows spaced far enough apart to allow easy movement in and out of the rows—is another option.

Chairs also enable more people to be seated in the same space. (Few people will sit on two chairs.) While a pew has room for ten people at 21 inches each (a comfortable width for a chair), on the average only eight will sit in the space. In most churches, changing to chairs increases the effective seating capacity by 10 to 20 percent.

A feature that can enhance the versatility of the ministry center is a partly or totally movable platform and movable choir risers. This allows for different sizes of choirs or musical groups and for various arrangements of staging—even in different parts of the room—for drama or orchestras. When there is no choir, the risers can be removed to eliminate the void of an empty choir loft.

Designing a lighting system for this space will require the ability of the best illumination engineer available. You will need equally expert help with acoustics and sound, since the acoustical treatment will have to be designed to work not from one direction but many. The most satisfactory sound system may be the movable "concert" type with several places around the room where controls, speakers, and microphones can be plugged in.

For total flexibility, front or back projection screens can also be movable rather than fixed. Electronic keyboards work better with this concept than a pipe organ (as much as I love pipe organs).

I used to believe that churches could not afford much storage space, because they needed the space for active use. What I've learned from growing churches is that multi-use spaces work well only when there are large storage spaces nearby so furniture, chairs, staging, and equipment can be moved in and out quickly.

While active storage should be adjacent to the room where the equipment is used, items not in active use should be stored in less costly areas.

Smaller Capacity

Two or three Sunday services are normal to many growing churches, plus, in some cases, services during the week.

While doing research for my masters degree in church design, I interviewed a Catholic priest. "How do you decide how many services to have and when to have them?" I asked.

He answered, "We have as many as are needed to serve the people, whenever they need them. For example, for people who have to work on Sunday we have a Saturday mass."

"How many have to attend before you'll schedule a service?" I asked.

His answer: "That's not important. We're here to serve."

When designing a new building, wouldn't it make sense at the same time to plan as many worship services as are needed at the times people need them? Compared with a single-service plan, this would make it possible to build a much smaller ministry center. Not only would this save money, but it would also bring people closer together and go far toward eliminating the problem of a meeting space that feels too big and impersonal. A moderately sized ministry center is also easier to subdivide into smaller meeting spaces than is a large auditorium, and it increases the variety of ministries for which the space can be used.

Just as multiple services make it possible to build a smaller ministry center, multiple sessions for Christian education make it possible to construct far less educational space. But building for high-intensity use does not simply mean building smaller. A facility designed for multiple Sunday services and multiple Sunday school sessions has special requirements.

In many churches that hold multiple services and Sunday school sessions, some people will go from worship to Sunday school while others are coming from Sunday school to worship. Some will arrive for the second service while others leave from the first service. This means that entryways and hallways in the multiservice building need to be designed to handle at least twice as much traffic as those in a single-service building. Parking will also need to be expanded with clearly marked entrances, exits, and traffic patterns, and more areas for loading and unloading passengers must be added.

Multiple services create yet one more special demand on a facility. In single-service churches people often linger in the worship area to visit after the service, standing between pews, in aisles, or in the back of the auditorium. A multiple-service church, however, must clear the worship area fairly quickly so arriving worshipers can enter. In addition, worshipers leaving the first service and those arriving for the second need a place where they can visit with each other. These needs and others can be met by another special feature designed specifically for the multi-use church: a fellowship foyer.

The Fellowship Foyer

The fellowship foyer is a room at least half the size of the ministry center (worship area). Like the traditional foyer, this is where people enter as they arrive for worship, and from here they enter the worship area. Unlike a traditional foyer, however, it is large enough to give worshipers leaving one service and those arriving for the next plenty of room to visit with each other and welcome visitors without blocking traffic.

Besides serving as a foyer, this room also fulfills all the functions of the traditional fellowship hall. A small serving kitchen to one side makes it ideal for serving light refreshments or even for banquets and receptions. This space is also well suited for conferences, recreational activities, work projects, and board meetings.

Like other multi-use space, the fellowship foyer needs ample storage for chairs, tables, equipment, and possibly staging. One option is to include movable walls to subdivide the room for use by smaller groups and classes. The fellowship foyer is an extremely versatile space that the people of the church will use almost every time they gather.

Space for Education

In the small church we design classrooms for a single teacher with a small number of students. While little rooms work well when classes are small, as the church grows, rows of little rooms no longer meet the church's educational needs.

A growing church will need multiple nurseries and large open spaces for children's classes that can be subdivided with sight breaks and movable supply storage units. It will need a single room large enough to hold the entire teen group. For its adult classes the church may need a few large rooms, many small meeting spaces, or a mixture of large and small spaces. As some classes grow and new ones are formed, the size of the meeting spaces needed is almost sure to keep changing. How can a church plan for such constant change?

The key is flexibility. Design space with movable walls that can be used to create spaces of various sizes. Or, design rooms of varying sizes so, for example, as the teen group grows, it can be moved into progressively larger rooms. Another solution to the same problem is to build temporary walls that can be removed to allow for growth and thereby expand the size of the room in stages. (See the appendix for a description of the kind and amount of educational space needed for nursery, children's classes, teens, and adults.)

Making the educational space multi-use means not only that it is used for multiple sessions of Sunday school but that it is available for a variety of functions all week long, such as a latchkey program and weeknight children's programs. To make weekday utilization practical, include movable, lockable supply cabinets for the workers and big storage rooms for the furniture and equipment the various programs use. This area also needs a serving kitchen, toilet facilities, and a directly controlled outside entrance that allows it to be used independently from the rest of the building.

Parking/Recreation

Another simple way to achieve multiple use is to use hard-surfaced parking lots for recreation. Space used for parking on Sunday can double as basketball, volleyball, and tennis courts during the week. Paved parking lots are also well suited to such games as shuffleboard, four square, and hopscotch. With a little fencing, part of a parking lot can double as a children's general play area.

The Ultimate Multi-use Space

A "sanctinasium" is a room that can be used for a wide range of functions from worship services to basketball. Cole Community Church, a large congregation in Boise, Idaho, has chosen to make a sanctinasium the center of its facility complex. Though basically a gymnasium, the facility includes a platform, stage, and baptistry so that it also serves as the worship area and fulfills a variety of other purposes.

The large congregation of Kansas City First Church of the Nazarene built a gymnasium with a movable platform. Both churches use their sanctinasiums for multiple church services, fellowship, recreation, their weekday schools, drama, music, lunch and dinner meetings, activities of teens, seniors, and other groups, plus community meetings. These rooms seldom lie idle. (See the appendix for more on the features of a sanctinasium.)

Except for offices, almost every room of your church facility can be designed for multiple use, enabling it to be used repeatedly on Sundays and intensively the other six days of the week. Such a design can reduce the amount of floor space needed per person by 40 to 50 percent and reduce the cost of construction proportionally. Because a multi-use building requires so much less of the congregation's time, money, and energy than does a traditional design, it can be one of the most valuable ministry tools your church could have for playing a key role in keeping the church's focus on people rather than buildings.

13

Designing Your Facilities for Outreach

Does the design of your facilities affect how successfully your congregation reaches out to others? While no building can do the work of outreach—buildings do not minister—a building can make a difference. Your building can erect barriers to outreach and service, or it can enhance the outreach ministries of your members and help to welcome people.

Take, for example, a building I designed for a church in a small Kansas town. The existing building was on a single residential lot with no parking space and almost no lawn or landscaping. There was nothing impressive about the facility. They really did need to build.

In contrast to the tiny, obscure site of their existing building, the site for the new building provided plenty of space, and the prime location gave me the opportunity to create a significant visual exposure. The focal point of the design was a sanctuary with a high-pitched roof. The lawn and trees framed the front of the sanctuary for visual emphasis. The one-story flat-roofed educational wing was kept low to emphasize the mass and vertical lines of the sanctuary. So that it would not distract from the building's beauty, I hid the parking behind the sanctuary and the educational wing.

Inside the attractive front entryway, a small foyer opened to the parking area on the back, the sanctuary on one side, and the educational wing on the other.

A modest budget required careful design to include all the needed areas. One money saver was that the pastor's study was in the parsonage so the building needed to include only one small office for records and supplies. The fellowship hall at the far end of the educational wing had a folding wall so it could be divided, and the worship overflow areas had folding walls so they could double as classrooms. At the time I designed this building in the early fifties folding walls were fairly new, so these were innovative features.

When the building was finished, the members were excited to have a new facility that provided everything they had asked for and more, all for a very reasonable cost. It was work in which I could take justifiable pride.

That building met the needs of its members then, and today it still meets their needs. What that building did not do, however, was provide a welcoming environment for newcomers or serve as an effective tool for outreach. It had not occurred to me at the time that it was even possible to design a building for outreach. Because I drew up plans with only the members' needs in mind, I unintentionally built into the design several barriers to outreach, all of them common in traditional church architecture.

Though I had made the front entry the focus of my design, it was not accessible from the parking area. Even behind the building I had provided no visitors' parking. As visitors entered the building, they found themselves in a foyer so small that if someone paused to greet them for more than a few seconds, they would block traffic.

On entering the sanctuary, visitors encountered a half-empty space that gave the impression that not many people cared to attend that church. This resulted from having built the sanctuary big enough to give the congregation room to double and having furnished it with fixed pews. Movable seating would have solved the empty-space problem by making it possible to remove the unneeded chairs.

Worshipers sat in a long, narrow room where they could see only the backs of other people's heads, rather than in a warm, welcoming space where they could see each others' faces and feel a sense of togetherness. Movable seating could have helped with this problem as well.

But the greatest barrier of all was that the church was not open for business except on Sundays and Wednesday evenings. Even when the church was open, this was not obvious to people passing by, because the parking and active entrance were hidden behind the building.

None of these shortcomings interfered with members' needs. The members still found ways to greet one another and make each other feel welcome. The members knew when the church was open for business. The members knew when and where they could reach the pastor any time they needed him. It was only visitors and those who sought the church's ministry during the week, perhaps with crisis needs, who encountered these barriers.

The motivating force of the growing church is serving others, both inside and outside the church body. Our buildings should express that purpose by being user friendly. This term covers a range of design goals from serving the handicapped to features that invite the "customer" in. Both inside and out, the facilities should say, "We're here to serve you." I helped a congregation in Bakersfield, California, develop a plan for a new church complex that illustrates several ways of doing this.

Invite People In Through What They See

The first way a facility can help to welcome people is to invite them in through what they see. The Bakersfield site plan seeks to do this through the following features:

Landscaped visitor parking is in front where it is always visible and available.

The offices are located in front with visitor and other parking areas adjacent to the weekday (office) entry. A canopy marks the entry, puts it in scale with people, and provides shelter, in this case mostly from the sun. This welcoming design leaves no doubt that this church is open for business all week long.

The church complex is planned so people can see people using the facility all week long. Outdoor terraces are placed where passersby can see people gathering and visiting, not in hidden courtyards.

Glass doors and walls at the large entryways to the fellowship foyer allow people outside to see people inside.

The entrances on both sides of the atriumlike fellowship foyer are serviced by driveways for unloading, with convenient parking nearby. A movable wall between the fellowship foyer and ministry center allows the two spaces to function together when needed.

The design is in scale with people; it uses sizes that make people feel comfortable, not overpowered, dominated, or awed. It avoids strong vertical elements, such as steeples, towers, and campaniles, in favor of horizontal lines and openings. Unlike the Kansas facility that made the sanctuary its visual focus, the large mass formed by the ministry center and fellowship foyer was placed in the center of the site behind the much smaller-scale administration unit.

At another church in the San Francisco area, the site plan includes a soccer field, a picnic grove, and a gym placed at the front of the site where traditionally the sanctuary would be located. A par exercise course is planned for the perimeter of the site for use by the community.

By making the church campus look inviting and open to the community, these congregations hope to announce to their neighbors before they say a word, "We're open for business. You're always welcome here. Membership not required."

Welcome People Throughout the Week

When we welcome visitors into our homes, we greet them at the door, on the porch, or in the yard. We invite them in, take their coats and hang them up, and offer them our most comfortable seating. We tell them where their children can be cared for and where the toilet facilities are. We offer them refreshments and do whatever else we can to make them feel at home.

If we truly want people to feel welcome in our churches, we will be no less intentional about welcoming visitors to our church offices during the week. But anyone who tries to exercise this kind of hospitality in a church office is likely to discover quickly that the building was not designed with hospitality in mind. Most churches offer guests little more than a few chairs in the secretarial work space.

To provide a welcoming environment to those who come to the church offices, I recommend a parlor or living-room-style reception and waiting room at the entrance to the staff office area. Here visitors can get information, rest, read, or visit, with refreshments available. This room also serves as a control point for entry to the building during the week. The key to making this space work is to staff it with volunteer greeters with big smiles. Outside of office hours this parlor can serve as a bride's room, a funeral family room, or even an evening meeting room if the design carefully considers traffic patterns.

If you are serious about extending a warm welcome to people who visit your office, consider providing a homelike reception parlor.

Welcome People to the Services

Your building should have one or more welcoming entrances for visitors to your services, entrances with a human scale that are convenient to visitor parking. I recommend a greeting alcove just inside the entrances, an area where greeters can invite visitors to step out of the flow of traffic, be comfortably seated, and be welcomed in a friendship zone designed for that purpose.

This alcove should be part of the large fellowship foyer described in chapter 12 through which people enter the worship area. This fellowship foyer is a key element in creating a welcoming environment, designed to promote fellowship among members and visitors before and after worship and other gatherings.

Traditionally the church has consigned "fellowship" to a room called a fellowship hall in the remotest part of the building. Fellowship, though, is not peripheral to the life of the church but essential. Without fellowship we have no church. To centrally locate a large fellowship foyer helps to integrate fellowship into the total life of the church rather than treat it as a separate, and perhaps optional, function of the body.

Of course, many churches whose buildings have traditional designs have been effective in reaching out to welcome new people into the fellowship, because the people have committed themselves to serving others. But if yours is that kind of a church, a church with a heart to serve, which kind of building would you rather have—one that erects obstacles to hospitality, or one that invites people in through what they see and offers a welcoming environment to all who come, whether during office hours or to services?

You can have a building that helps you say, "We're here to serve. Come on in."

Conclusion

14

Releasing the Church to Change the World

Sometimes I ask a congregation, "How much do you expect to spend on your next building program? What might happen if instead of spending it on a new building you raised that same amount in cash and pledges to minister to the needs of people right here in your own community?"

Imagine with me. Imagine that the year is 2030 and that over the intervening years thousands of churches have dared to accept this challenge. They have adopted the principle of use: They will not build any new facilities until they are using their existing facilities as fully as possible. It has become commonplace for churches to have not just double worship services but three, four, even five services. Virtually every square foot of space in every church building has been designed or remodeled so it can be used for a variety of purposes all week long. As a result, churches grow to two, three, even four times the size they once did before they need additional buildings.

Imagine that these same churches have long since converted from debt financing to provision financing. Because they no longer have interest expense, the amount they spend on construction is only about a third of what it would have been if they had borrowed the money.

Now imagine that these churches have taken all the money saved by not building unnecessary buildings and by not paying interest and have invested that amount in ministering to the needs of people in their own neighborhoods or nearby communities. What would these churches be like now?

Imagine a church in a small farm community where restless youth look for something to do on Saturday night, where people often grow lonely as they grow older, where limited economic opportunities leave hard-working families helpless during economic downturns, where the everybody-knows-everybody-else's-business atmosphere compounds the pain of being fired, of chemical dependency, of divorce. Once such a church has redirected its focus from building to meeting the needs of people, how will the church have changed? How will the changed church have changed the community?

Think of a church in an affluent suburban neighborhood. After they drew the line on building they redirected their time, energy, and money into reaching out to the needs of those who lived there. All kinds of support groups sprang up: AA, AlAnon, Divorce Recovery, Cancer Recovery. Members developed ministries to help restore hurting marriages and help parents re-establish relationships with alienated children. The church began to provide finances and volunteers for a variety of ministries in a nearby low-income neighborhood. Throughout the community the church became known as a group of people who have their fingers firmly on the pulse of the community's needs and who reach out creatively and compassionately to meet those needs.

Or imagine an inner city congregation whose limited resources are straining to respond to poverty, single-parent homes, child abuse, chemical dependency, unsafe housing, and despair. Most such churches already have a long record of creative and intensive use of facilities. But what would happen in this congregation if churches from surrounding suburbs redirected hundreds of thousands of dollars that traditionally would have been spent on church buildings to minister to these desperate needs?

Imagining three such churches is easy. After all, churches like these are around, and we all admire them. But now imagine that by the year 2030 half the churches in your city or town look like this. No, they are not all cut out of the same mold. Each congregation has unique ministries that grow out of the needs of its neighbors and the gifts and callings of its members. Yet they all share this in common: They no longer consider bigger or more impressive buildings to be signs of success. All that matters is to minister to people's needs by the power of Christ.

If that were true of just half the churches of your community, how would your community be changed? Can you imagine it? What new or expanded services would be available to the elderly? To the unemployed? To abused children and those who abuse them? How would life be different for single teenage moms in your community? How many more promising young people from underprivileged homes would receive technical training or go to college?

What new opportunities would be available to those who seek drug rehabilitation? For students who need extra tutoring? For the medically underserved? For those living in substandard housing? For those needing job training or financial counseling?

If all these tangible expressions of caring had sprung up in your community, some from your church, most from others, what differences might you see in the juvenile delinquency rate? In the crime rate? In the unemployment rate? In the divorce rate?

What would it have meant for the people in your congregation to be personally involved, week after week, in compassionate ministries to hurting people? To have seen God work through them to bring comfort and healing? To have encountered God in those they served, and to have been surprised again and again by being ministered to in the act of ministering? To have worked hand in hand in ministries to the community with Christians of many denominations—Baptists and Roman Catholics, Nazarenes and United Methodists, Assemblies of God and Presbyterians— all united by love of God and love of neighbor?

If half the churches in your community made the commitment to redirect three-fourths of their construction funds to meet the needs of people right in your own community, and all these ministries grew out of that commitment, how would that change how your community saw the church? How much more open to the gospel might the unchurched be? What effect might that have on the size of the churches in your town?

Now, multiply that image by thousands. What if the transformation you have just envisioned for your own community were duplicated in every community in your state or province? What if half of all the churches in every town in the United States and Canada caught this vision and determined never again to let buildings become their focus, not even temporarily? How would our society be changed?

It's difficult to imagine anything approaching this without envisioning one of the greatest revivals of all time. By the millions our neighbors would be struck with the truth that Christianity is not some special interest group seeking to promote its own success but a radically caring community of people who have tapped into a power that can meet their deepest needs and change their lives.

No more powerful force in the war on drugs would exist than the power of the church. There would be no more powerful force in the battle against unemployment than the church. Politicians in Ottawa and Washington would talk about what to do with the "church dividend," the hundreds of billions of dollars no longer needed for government social programs because the church once again was taking its rightful place in meeting the needs of people, and doing so far more effectively than the government ever had been able to do. This would echo the days of the early Christian church.

Had the churches of the first and second centuries focused on buildings, such a witness as theirs never would have taken place. But because they focused on meeting the needs of people by God's power, the world sat up and took notice.

There is no reason that the church today cannot recover the vitality of that early church. Our nations can be changed by God's love. Your city or town can be transformed. But it will never happen on the scale it needs to happen until we change the way we think about church buildings, until we realize that building buildings is not the work of the church, that at best buildings are only tools that can help us with the work of the church to meet people's needs through the power and love of Christ.

Appendix

How to Write a Program of Needs for Your Church Facility

Your architect cannot design in a vacuum. Without knowing the specific needs of your church, some architects will rely on traditional designs developed for the maintenance (nongrowing) church, designs that do not take into account the special design requirements of a fast-growing congregation. Traditionally, architects are not trained to design for the growing church, so it is up to the church growth committee, or whatever you call the group responsible to plan your facility needs, to give your architect clear direction. (For help on how to form this committee, review chapter 11.)

The tool you create to direct your architect is called a program of needs. This is a written document based on realistic projections of growth. It itemizes facility needs and desires for all the functions of your church: worship and other large group gatherings, fellowship, education, administration, recreation, and parking. It describes how different parts of the building are to relate to each other, to entrances, to parking, and to streets. It includes any equipment, furnishings, or other special requirements that the committee wants incorporated into the design. It specifies design needs that grow out of the liturgy of your faith tradition or denomination.

As a part of writing your program, visit at least one or two fast-growing churches, preferably of your own denomination, that have built recently. Find out which aspects of their facilities work well and which do not, and incorporate what you learn into your plan.

Keep in mind that the growth committee does not design a building; it only defines what it wants the building to do. It is the architect's job to design a building to meet all these needs. Even so, preparation of a program of needs is a demanding task and in some cases will require the help of a professional—a church facilities consultant or architect who understands the special needs of growing churches.

The following outline can guide you in drawing up your church's program of needs. It incorporates features specifically designed to meet the needs of the growing church—high-intensity multiple use of space, and features intended to facilitate outreach. If you plan for an entirely new facility, you can incorporate as many of these features as you wish. If you remodel or build an addition, you will still be able to adopt many of these concepts, though with some limitations. Even if you meet in rented facilities, you should be able to come up with significant ways to improve upon your use and configuration of space to allow for growth.

After becoming familiar with the following outline, the church growth committee should consider individually each of the seven areas described.

> Which of the concepts described both below and in the referenced portions of the book are practical and desirable for your congregation? Go through the book and highlight each of the features you want to incorporate into your design.

Which concepts are not practical or desirable for your situation? Go through the book and mark each of these items with an *X*. Then, as a committee, develop and write out an alternate plan for these aspects of your program of need.

Finally, give your architect your highlighted copy of this book along with the supplemental plans you have written. Together, these make up your program of need. Of course, if you prefer you can combine the highlighted features from the book and your supplemental plans into a single document for the architect. If you use any of the special features advocated in this book, however, it is essential that you have your architect read the book so he or she will clearly understand the purpose of those features and how they are to relate to the rest of the building.

Ministry Center

I recommend that the growing church build not a traditional sanctuary but a ministry center. Refer to chapter 12 for a description of how this multi-use space can work.

If you choose to create a ministry center, you have two major decisions to make. First, how many services do you plan to hold? Your answer to this question will largely determine the size of this space. Second, what functions will you use this space for? Your answer to this question will determine your needs for equipment, movable versus fixed staging, lighting, acoustical treatment and sound system, and active storage adjacent to the room.

Key to making the ministry center concept work is the use of movable church chairs for seating. Church chairs are stored by stacking, not folding. They are upholstered, more comfortable than pews, have wood or steel frames, and are designed to gang together. They will probably cost more than pews but are worth it, because they increase your seating capacity as well as make the room usable for multiple ministries throughout the week.

They are available with book racks, communion cup holders, and envelope racks.

If your church wishes to consider the sanctinasium option for a ministry center (see end of chapter 12), you should be aware of the following requirements for making such a facility workable:

A gym–type carpeted floor.

Acoustical treatment for speaking and music.

A sound system designed for this space, with a movable console.

A dual lighting system: for recreation, high-intensity lighting; for worship and other uses, appropriate lighting that can be dimmed, together with theatrical lighting and controls for the platform area.

Large active storage rooms for equipment and furniture.

Preparation rooms for drama and other programs.

Dressing rooms for recreation.

The key to making a sanctinasium work is to design it primarily to satisfy the needs of worship and other services, including the gym functions, rather than to design a typical gym and then use it for worship.

Fellowship Foyer

For the growing church I recommend a fellowship foyer that combines the functions of the traditional foyer and the traditional fellowship hall. It is often practical to build a fellowship foyer as an addition to an existing building. When a church wishes to go to multiple services in a building designed for single services, the addition of a fellowship foyer may be essential to make multiple services practical. For the multi-use and traffic flow functions of the fellowship foyer, see chapter 12. For the welcoming and outreach functions of the fellowship foyer, see chapter 13.

If you choose to include a fellowship foyer in your design, a major decision you face is whether to include a movable wall system so that in addition to its use as a foyer and fellowship hall some or all of the space can be used for small groups and classes.

Educational Functions

The kind of space needed for educational use varies with the age group. Modify the following recommendations to meet the needs of your church.

Nursery. If the church serves young families, careful planning of the nursery area should be a high priority. For many parents with nursery-age children an excellent nursery and staff is the single greatest factor in choosing a church home.

The nursery should be easily accessible from the visitors' parking and not too close to the ministry center. Provide extra corridor space at the entrances to the nursery rooms so parents can pick up their children without entering the rooms.

Design separate spaces for toddlers, crawlers, and crib babies, with each room having a maximum capacity of twelve to fifteen children plus workers. If possible, provide a sleeping room just off the crib room that is completely visible to crib room workers. A room where mothers can care for and feed their children should have its own entrance so mothers need not go through the nursery.

Equip each room with individual cubicles for each child's personal things, including diaper bags, just inside the door. Each room should have an adult-size toilet, counter, and sink. Have a storage closet for toys, supplies, folding play pens, and other equipment in each room.

Children. While rows of small rooms work well for children's classes in small churches, in the larger church large flexible spaces are more practical. Movable sight breaks and storage units on wheels can be arranged to subdivide open spaces for age groupings. A single-age group can grow to thirty or forty in one room if the adult-to-student ratio is appropriate for the age.

The master-teacher/worker approach is a practical way to staff such classes. Each room is supervised by a master teacher who is assisted by one worker for each four to five preschoolers, each five to six primaries, or each eight to ten older children. Workers serve as care givers at tables or in activity groups and help to maintain control when the whole group is assembled.

Design of this kind of classroom should include excellent sound absorption, a work counter with a sink and drinking fountain, and a toilet facility so children need not leave the room or area.

Teens. There appears to be no upper limit to the size of the junior high or senior high departments. The bigger the group, the better the teens seem to like it. Large churches that have tried to divide the teens (into two sessions of Sunday school, for example) have usually found it does not work; the teens all gravitate to one session. The best way to accommodate a growing teen ministry, therefore, seems to be to provide larger rooms as the teen group grows. This makes planning facilities for a growing youth group a challenge.

One solution is to use a movable sound-wall system. Another is to plan walls that can be removed for growth into adjacent space. (You can build and remove inexpensive gypsum walls several times before their cost will equal the cost of a sound-wall system.) Or you can plan a variety of room sizes and move the group to ever-larger rooms as needed. Whichever solution you choose, it is critical to design the room for high decibel levels (what adults call noise).

Like other parts of the building, the teen meeting areas should be designed for intensive use during the week. This requires large storage rooms for the various furnishings and equipment used in youth ministry. An outside entrance to the area, a serving kitchen, and toilet facilities are all important to weekday utilization.

Successful use of a gymnasium as the primary meeting space for teens is difficult to achieve. It may be possible by using gym-type carpet, acoustical treatment, a movable sound system, a dual lighting system, plus enough storage to make a gym work. But, be aware of the limitations.

Adults. Facility requirements for adult classes vary from church to church. One congregation had only two adult classes of several hundred each, both taught lecture style by master teachers. Another church tried to keep classes in a range of thirty to sixty so each would function as a "congregation" within the larger church. The more common pattern is to have a variety of class sizes and different styles of teaching. If you have any special classes that require something other than the usual rectangular room, the needs of those classes must figure into your design. The building plan should follow the teaching plan to be used, not vice versa.

Space Allowances. The following space allowances are in common use and can guide you in determining your space needs for education. Teachers and workers are counted along with their students. Space allowances are based on *average* attendance and allow room for 20 percent growth and occasional higher attendance. Area is based on wall-to-wall measurements.

Age Group	Range of Needed Space
Nursery, preschool, and kindergarten	30 sq. ft. per person
	35 sq. ft. with large equipment
	25 sq. ft. minimum
Children	
Lower grades	25 sq. ft. each
	20 sq. ft. minimum
Upper grades	20 sq. ft. each
	15 sq. ft. minimum
Teens	
Class only	15 sq. ft. each (with tables)
Total multi-use	20 sq. ft. each
Adults	
At tables	15 sq. ft. each
Lecture class	12 sq. ft. each
	10 sq. ft. minimum

The total building area needed for classrooms, walls, corridors, toilets, mechanical, janitor, and storage is close to 50 square feet per person, based on average attendance and single use of the facility.

Study the space utilization of your present classes based on average attendance and adjust the above allowances to your specific methods and needs. The space needed per person is determined primarily by the method of teaching, type of furniture, and how the furniture is arranged. Identify space wasters—large tables with seating on just one side, a large room with seating only around the walls, or big overstuffed divans and chairs.

A note on tables: Buy the best, strongest folding tables available; it saves money in the long run. Buy six-foot tables (maximum size) so one person can fold and stack them. They are the best size for children's classes, seating six per table plus the teacher and a guest if needed. This size also gangs together best.

Make sure all tables are adjustable in height so they can be changed quickly from children's use to adults' and back again.

Administration

The most important requirement for administrative space is to gather all professional ministry staff and support staff offices into a single administrative suite. This is important for efficiency, teamwork, and accountability, as well as to enable all staff members to be easily available to the public—a key component of being open for business. The offices should be close to work areas, a copy machine, a conference room, and other facilities used in common.

The offices should be in the front part of the building, highly visible, with convenient parking, easy to enter, and totally user friendly. The entryway should be designed to say "welcome." If possible, the church that is determined to offer a welcoming environment to those it serves should provide a comfortable, parlorlike hospitality area for office visitors just inside the weekday (office) entrance. Chapter 13 describes this feature in more detail.

For planning purposes use a ratio of one professional ministry staff member per 150 people being served, unless you have developed your own ratio. Keep in mind that staff is added ahead of the next growth phase. A ratio of one support staff member for every two professional staff members is minimum if the professionals are to spend their time doing what they are educated and trained for rather than doing work secretaries can do faster and better. The facility plan must provide for future expansion of the administrative area as growth requires, either by changing the function of adjacent space to administration or by constructing an addition to the building.

One facility need almost always overlooked is space for lay ministry staff. Every growing congregation has members willing to serve in support roles. They need places to work with the assistance and supervision of the professional and support staff. This work space may include telephones for outreach and follow-up, an area for lay counseling, or work space to prepare mailings. The church that takes the ministry of the laity seriously enough to provide office space and equipment for its lay ministers is more likely to be a growing church.

For more specific suggestions on how to make your administrative space "open for business," review chapter 7.

Recreation

In the forties and fifties many churches said, "We want to minister to the youth of our church and community, so design us a *youth center.*" In the sixties and seventies the big thrust was to build a *recreation center.* In the eighties the *family-life center* was where the action was. I wonder what name we will invent next to describe what we build, because for all of the above we have built *gymnasiums.*

The motives behind this were all great, but most of these churches built buildings to house nonexistent ministries. They assumed that if they built the buildings, people would use them. But most of the time the buildings lay unused.

Consider building a gymnasium only if the church already has a strong, successful ministry that uses recreation and if other facilities are not available. Do a careful cost effectiveness study before deciding on a gymnasium. To be cost effective it must be a multi-use facility, and that requires a first-class, expensive building. (See the discussion of educational space for teens earlier in this appendix for the basic features needed in a multipurpose gymnasium.) A bare-bones gym is a poor investment, because it will have very limited use.

I have yet to witness a church using a recreational program as an effective ministry for outreach. I have seen some limited success with softball and basketball. The potential is there for a ministry, but remember: Create the ministry first, then build the facility.

In considering recreational needs, keep in mind that paved parking can, for minimal cost, be designed for basketball, volleyball, tennis, and other recreational uses.

Parking

Growth is stopped by the shortage of parking more often than by any other single facilities requirement. A ratio of one car for every 2.5 people works in most areas. To find out what the car-to-people ratio is in your church, count all the people in the building (including children, of course) and all the cars parked at the church. In your planning, assume that the ratio will go down and require proportionally more parking spaces in the future. A ratio of one car for every 2 people applies in some affluent suburbs.

Without landscaping, you can park about 120 cars per acre; about 100 per acre with landscaping. With compact spaces the ratio may be increased. Most cities and counties have specific parking space requirements, such as landscaping and control of water runoff.

When you consider parking options, particularly at existing sites, don't forget to consider alternative approaches: remote parking with shuttle service, stacked parking, getting multiple use out of parking space by having multiple services. Remember that worship and education classes cannot be held at the same time unless there is enough parking for both. (See chapter 5 to review parking options.)

External Appearance of Facility

The outward appearance of your facility, including the scale of the building, location of offices, location of parking, location of recreational facilities, entryways, and landscaping all combine to make a statement to the community. They can say, "We're number one," an intimidating message; or they can say, "We're open for business, and you're always welcome."

Study chapter 13 as you consider how to design the appearance of your building, parking, and grounds to express the message you truly want to communicate.

Once your growth committee has written up your program of needs in the above seven areas (plus other areas required by your church's particular needs, such as music rehearsal), you are ready to show your program to your architect. Since your architect may not have been trained in many of the concepts described in this book—particularly high-intensity multi-use design and a building designed primarily for others rather than for the members—you will need to employ an architect who is flexible and who enjoys developing innovative solutions to architectural challenges.

By basing his or her work on the detailed program of needs your committee has created guided by this outline, your architect should be able to design a facility almost ideally suited to your congregation's needs and goals.

Notes

Chapter 1: Confessions of a Surprised Architect

1. Richard Foster, *The Freedom of Simplicity* (San Francisco: Harper & Row, 1981), 153–4.

Chapter 2: Can Buildings Kill Church Growth?

1. Throughout this book, names of congregations have been changed except when the town where the church is located is named.

Chapter 8: Good Intentions Are Not Enough

1. Larry Burkett, *Should Churches Borrow Money?* (Tucker, Georgia: Christian Financial Concepts, 1978), pamphlet.

2. Virgil Vogt, *Treasure in Heaven* (Ann Arbor, Michigan: Servant Books, 1982), 92–93.

Chapter 10: Turning Church Spending Right Side Up

1. Eberhard Arnold, *The Early Christians,* trans. and ed. Society of Brothers (1970, 1972; Grand Rapids: Baker Book House, 1979), 18–19.

Acknowledgments

I wish to thank first of all my wife, Sally, who has been a co-laborer with me in our consulting ministry since it began in 1980. In our work with churches her gifts have consistently compensated for certain of my weaknesses. As a partner on the consulting team she has played a critical role in developing many of the concepts that appear in these pages, and has, of course, been deeply involved in shaping the manuscript.

Since 1987 Eddy Hall has been our as-told-to writer who organized and interpreted our experiences for publication in professional journals for pastors and denominational magazines. In the writing of this book he continued in that role, sometimes pulling out of me more than I knew I had to give. I appreciate not only Eddy's writing skills but also his vision for church renewal, which enabled him to contribute considerable original material to the book as he also drew on his own study of Scripture and his personal experience.

I want to thank James N. Posey, who introduced me to the principles of biblical finance on which part 3 of this book is based, and who provided encouragement—and on two occasions office space—for the writing process. I thank Shirley Posey who volunteered her able services as proofreader and copy editor of the manuscript. Elizabeth Ketner, my mother-in-law, allowed us to set up office in her home and extended warm hospitality during the writing of the last fourth of the book, which I enjoyed and appreciated. My thanks also to Rebecca Laird for critiquing the book proposal and making valuable suggestions.

Many people contributed to this book by influencing my thinking with their books, tapes, or personal contact. Principal among these are Howard Chambers through his pastoral work; Ray Stedman through his writings, tapes, and speeches; Win Arn and Charles Arn through their writing and seminars; Peter Wagner and Carl George through their writing and teaching; Joseph Aldridge through his writing; Richard Foster through his writing; and Larry Burkett through his writing.

Most of all, I thank God, who called me into such a challenging ministry when I could not even conceive of what he was leading me into, and who gave me the opportunity to learn from the hundreds of churches I have worked with the many exciting concepts and practical ideas I could have learned no other way.

Ray Bowman Consulting, Inc.
4526 Sentinel Rock Terrace
Larkspur, CO 80118-8905
(303) 681-3543